PENTAGON PRESS

COMMITTED TO SERVE THE ARMED FORCES

ROOKS AND KNIGHTS

ROOKS AND KNIGHTS

Civil–Military Relations in India

R Chandrashekhar

Foreword by

Lt Gen Vinod Bhatia, PVSM, AVSM, SM (Retd)

Director, Centre for Joint Warfare Studies

CENTRE FOR JOINT WARFARE STUDIES (CENJOWS)

PENTAGON PRESS

ROOKS AND KNIGHTS: *Civil–Military Relations in India*
R Chandrashekhar

ISBN 978-81-8274-923-8

First Published in 2017

Published by
PENTAGON PRESS
206, Peacock Lane, Shahpur Jat
New Delhi-110049
Phones: 011-64706243, 26491568
Telefax: 011-26490600
email: rajan@pentagonpress.in
website: www.pentagonpress.in

Printed at Avantika Printers Private Limited.

To

My Wife

Tripta

For her enduring patience and support that made this book happen.

CONTENTS

Lt Gen Vinod Bhatia, PVSM, AVSM, SM (Retd)
Director

Tele : 011-23006535, 23792446
Ascon : 35681
Telefax : 011-23792444
Email : ptrsix@gmail.com
cenjows@yahoo.com

Centre for Joint Warfare Studies
(CENJOWS)
Kashmir House
Rajaji Marg
New Delhi-110011

FOREWORD

1. The Centre for Joint Warfare Studies (CENJOWS) was raised at the initiative of Ministry of Defence with mandate to promote integration as a synergistic enabler for the growth of integrated National Power and provide alternatives in all dimensions of its applications through focused research and debate, Since its raising in 2007, CEMJOWS has endeavoured to examine joint warfare and synergy in their entirety. 'Rooks and Knights Civil Military Relations in India' is one of the endeavours in the regard.

2. Conceived initially as a Project to understand the synamics of the control mechanisms for the Armed Forces in India, the depth and detail of research assiduously carried out by Shri R Chandrashekhar, a Senior Fellow with CENJOWS merited his efforts being placed in the public domain to enable those in Government, Military and others interested in the subject to readily access and further their understanding of this interesting subject. As Director CENJOWS, it is my privilege to commend the author's yeoman efforts. The book gives an unparalleled insight into the various facets of civil-military relationship from sublime to the ridiculous. It makes an interesting and educative reading for military and civilians alike to comprehend the dynamics of this often cursed and warped relationship, effective by exception.

3. CENJOWS is also happy to collaborate with M/s Pentagon Press in the production of 'Rooks and Knights'.

(Vinod Bhatia)
Lt Gen (Retd)
Dir CENJOWS

INTRODUCTION

The edifice of a democratic form of Government rests on the plank of effective civilian control, not merely of its military but of the nation's security apparatus. The relationship between the nation's Civilian Authorities and its Armed Forces is therefore a determining index to ascertain the strength of its tethering to democratic values.

Civilian control over the Armed Forces is exercised through manifold 'connecting threads' which relate to several aspects of functional and administrative control, oversight and decision making ranging from stipulating their role, mission purpose, aspects of their budgeting, procurement, structure and not the least, the position of the Armed Forces in the body politic of the nation.

A large volume of academic literature is available that discusses the relative 'superiority' of the democratic system over other systems of government. One such interesting study titled *Democracy and Battlefield Military Effectiveness* (by Dan Reiter of the Department of Political Science, Emory University and Allan C. Stam III of the Department of Political Science Yale University) explores the question of 'whether the armies of democratic states fight with higher military effectiveness on the battlefield'. The Study seeks to test whether the 'higher legitimacy of democratic states' spurs 'superior individual soldiering' and whether 'democratic militaries are likely to have higher organizational efficacy' through a comprehensive set of major battles from 1800 to 1982, using data compiled by the Historical Evaluation and Research Organization. The authors find that the armies of democratic states 'tend to fight with marginally better logistics, substantially better initiative, and superior leadership'. Most pertinently, they also observe that 'all three of these advantages dwindle as wars lengthen' In their interpretation, 'although soldiers are not more willing to die for democratic governments, the emphasis on individual initiative in democratic culture generates important advantages on the battlefield'.[1]

There are no universally applicable yardsticks to determine the extent and nature of civilian control of the Armed Forces in a democratic state. Each nation per force develops and follows its own model that it considers best suited to its own circumstances. The geographical size of the nation, its local and regional geopolitics, the obtaining security environment, its capacity to allot resources are all factors in the evolution of the 'control' mechanism followed. The one distinct and inevitable feature is that the reigns of control of the military rest wholly and squarely in the hands of the duly elected Civilian Authority.

Once this overarching stipulation is fulfilled, there are, within its scope, various factors that influence the obtaining Civil–Military 'balance' at any point of time. Some of these are charismatic and visionary leadership (on either or both sides) and the role Armed Forces are expected to or are playing at that time and public expectations and support for them. These factors are in turn subject to influence by perceptions carried in the media and pressure from civil society activists. That the Armed Forces in a democratic form of Government are an instrument of State Policy is a 'given'. It is their primary role to execute directions from the civilian political authority and with alacrity, efficiency and professionalism. The Armed Forces are not to doubt or question why a direction has so been given. That remains the sole purview of the Civilian political class.

The other side to this coin is that on its part, the political class must be in the full know of the capabilities and limitations of the Armed Forces. They must have a candid appreciation of what is achievable by its Forces, the obtaining state of its personnel, their morale and the wherewithal provided to them to execute their tasks. An aspect of Civil–Military Relations (CMR) is existence of formal mechanisms and structures to make objective assessments and to what extent the Military itself is integrated into the process of appraisal of the 'State of the Forces'.

This book endeavours to examine the dynamics of decision making on both the 'Civil' and the 'Military' side of the balance and to identify such areas and aspects where systemic or structural changes need to be effected, if at all, to existing arrangements. There have been several detailed studies conducted on the subject of CMR in India. An overwhelming majority of these, however, have been conducted by the Armed Forces Officers. Not much literature is available that elucidates the Civilian side perspective. 'Rooks and Knights' is a modest effort to collate and view perspectives on both sides through a single prism with the intent to identify and address fault lines, both extant and likely to emerge in future.

While on the high principles of political philosophy its democratic traditions undoubtedly is a cherished jewel of Indian polity, on a more practical and mundane plane, a robust national Security apparatus is as much imperative to preserve and safeguard these traditions.

The Civil–Military debate in India is in essence one that seeks the fine balance that ensures both: an effective civilian control as also an effective and efficient national security apparatus.

Only then can true democracy prevail both in spirit and substance.

NOTE

1. Reiter, Dan and Allan C. Stam III, 'Democracy and Battlefield Military Effectiveness', *Journal of Conflict Resolution*, June 1998, pp. 259–77.

CHAPTER 1

THEORIES ON CIVIL–MILITARY RELATIONS

THEORIES ON CIVIL–MILITARY RELATIONS

> *'Make security subordinate to the larger purposes of a nation, rather than the other way around. The purpose of the military is to defend society, not to define it'.*
>
> – Lindsay Kohn[1]

The primacy of the civil control being inviolate, the relationship between the civil democratic government and its armed forces, a body of professionals, hence requires fine balance. The factors that mark and maintain that balance, areas of decision making by the civil government, the cross flow of information, inputs, advice and counsel in deciding roles and tasks, the responsibility for success or failure in their execution are the various tipping points in this balance.

Each Nation develops its own syntax of defining conditions that vary with the size of the nation and its military, its level of development and ability to provide for military wherewithal and perhaps most importantly, the intensity of the social and cultural milieu with which its people view and are impacted by the security issues the nation faces.

Briefly recapitulating the essence of various theories propounded on Civil–Military Relations by academic and social scientists would form a useful backdrop to examining the CMR and the control mechanism as has evolved in India.

The 'Institutional' Theory

Samuel Huntington's *The Soldier and the State* published in 1957 and regarded as the seminal literature on Civil–Military Relations, describes the diversion between the liberal 'civil' and the conservative 'military' as being two worlds with their own values, traditions, concerns and work ethos. The theory recognises that the two have different roles, the 'civil' having responsibility to set the objectives for military action and the 'military' to achieve these objectives. The 'control' of the 'military' insofar as setting its tasks and enabling it adequately to achieve them is of the 'civil'. Once the 'civil' has defined and stated the objectives, however, it is the 'military' which has to apply its professional acumen and capabilities to achieve them. The 'professionalism' of the military enable it to submit to the control of the Civil and recognises its role as the executor of civil decisions.

There are two defining factors Samuelson emphasises upon. First, that the professionalism that drives the military is of its 'Officer Corps', who have the requisite, training and experience to reflect a mature understanding of this subtle divide and not other enlisted troops. Second, the 'Civil' keeps apart from interfering or infringing on the decisions of the 'Military' in executing its role. The degree of control of the Civil over the Military is upon what the theory rests. Too much control may impact professional decision making and lead to operational failure. Too little control on the other hand may result in the Military becoming too powerful and assuming a larger than envisaged role.

The balance between the two is achieved through what Samuelson states as 'Objective Civilian Control'. This 'objectivity' is in turn guided by the ideology of the Civil Government whether liberal, conservative, fascist or dictatorial and the legal and administrative mechanisms in place to effect control over the Military.

In a variation to the Huntington Model, Michael Desch has theorised of a 'thin permeable layer' between 'political ends' and 'military means'[2]. The Military enjoys maximum autonomy in the operational and technical realms but the subordination to the civil on political aspects and grand strategy is total. This thin layer permits exceptional, though limited room for either to flow into the realm of the other, i.e. for civilian intervention in the area of the military as also, where required, for the military to act politically.

The 'Convergence' Theory

Propounded by Morris Janowitz in his book *The Professional Soldier* published in 1960, this theory accepts a liberal 'Civil' and a conservative 'Military as being two distinct worlds. Janowitz argues that over time, either a 'civilianisation of the Military or a militarisation of the Civil does occur though certain basic characteristics are retained by each'. Janowitz considered that the 'dilution' of conservatism of the military would reduce the 'attitudinal distance' between the two worlds and result in better Civilian control of the Military.

In a nuclear age, the role of the Military according to Janowitz was changing from one to be called out in an emergency to that more akin to a 'police force' required to either provide strategic deterrence' or participate in limited operations at an international level. To enable efficient execution of the redefined role, the Civil would per force require to work in close interaction with the Military so that the latter has required clarity on the objective and of the force required to be applied in achieving it, thus highlighting the inevitable 'convergence' the theory propounds.

The Agency Theory

Peter Feaver in his treatise *Armed Servants: Agency, Oversight, and Civil–Military Relations* postulated on the lines of Huntington that Policy was the prerogative of the Civil and the Military was the 'Agent', a subordinate, which executed the tasks called upon to achieve the desired ends of that policy.

The theory derives from the failure of the Military in the Vietnam War which is widely believed to have been 'lost in Washington DC' due to needless Civilian meddling in regard to application of military force, especially restraints on its use. Military professionalism that Huntington cherished is one in which the Civilian leadership provided 'objective control' and thereafter stepped back to allow the Military to carry out its tasks.

Moreover, in carrying out its role, Feaver added that the Military may either 'work' or 'shirk'. In circumstances where civil control is excessive and intrusive, 'shirking' by the Military may affect national objectives. From the Military 'agent's' perspective, shirking would be inversely proportional to the costs of punishment. He considered his theory to be different from both the 'Institutional' and of 'Convergence' with the role of the Military defined as that of an 'Executive Agent' with limits to the extent Civil authority would apply the levers of control.

Concordance Theory

All three theories discussed above presume that the Civil and Military are necessarily apart and separate playing out their respective roles as determinants of policy and executors of the same. Rebecca Schiff in her treatise *The Military and Domestic Politics: A Concordance Theory of Civil–Military Relations* does not consider such a state of exclusivity as necessary and has offered an alternate theory of 'Concordance' between the three cardinal stakeholders, i.e. the Political Class, the Military and the Citizens in general, to cooperate to safeguard and promote the national cause.[3] This cooperation, which aims to curtail the prospects of domestic military intervention, is focused on four areas which have to be addressed conjointly to enable a harmonious and conflict-free relationship.

These focus areas are the political decision making process, the social composition of the officer corps, the recruitment of personnel into the military and the military methods and 'style' of conduct. Rebecca Schiff applied her concepts to developments in various countries, including post-Independence India and Pakistan to validate them.

THE RELEVANCE OF THE CMR THEORIES IN THE INDIAN CONTEXT

The question next arises as to which of these theories applies to the Indian scenario. The defining aspects need to be highlighted at the very outset. First, there is indeed a need for exclusivity between the Civil and the Military in India (which is the mainstay of discussion in this book). Second, and significantly, the Military in India has no direct institutional presence at the highest echelons of strategic policy formulation or decision making.

The three Services Headquarters remain largely as 'Attached Offices' of the Ministry of Defence. There are no Services officers posted to the Ministry of Defence and most pertinently, the Service Chiefs find no mention at all in the Allocation of Business Rules 1961 and they are not part of the administrative superstructure of the Government. There is undoubtedly, an 'Agency' system in place.

The 'civil' side perspective on the applicability of these theories in the Indian context was articulated by Shri NN Vohra, erstwhile Defence and Home Secretary to the Government of India, later Principal Secretary to the Prime Minister and presently the Hon'ble Governor of J&K and one of India's legendary bureaucrats, who, while delivering the Annual USI National Lecture 2013, put it bluntly that **"Western theories of Civil Military Relations have no applicability to India"**. With its origins predating either Huntington or Janowitz, the evolution of civil military relations in India has not been scripted to comply with any one or other theory. It stands by itself, unique and self-grown.

Retrofitting these theories to the Indian scenario however, throws up interesting comparisons. It is 'Concordance' that apparently underlies the aspirations of the Indian Armed Forces. National Security is the prime area of their professional focus. They possess an in-depth understanding of the relevant issues distilled with due thought and deliberation. Combined with their knowledge on the application of force, its consequences and implications, there is in the Armed Forces a reservoir of professional inputs to support credible decision making.

The Civilian, be it the Political Class or Bureaucracy, notwithstanding their exposure to and understanding of military and security issues being largely for the durations they tenant office, have yet so far adopted and even enforced the 'Agency' Theory with the Military, keeping it both apart and subordinate. It is a different aspect as to whether even the sharpest generalist can grasp all the nuances of a complex, nuclearised strategic environment and the extent to which the Civilian class is dependent upon that very Military to obtain a credible understanding of emergent issues. 'Inputs' are no doubt sought from the Services on specific matters on the agenda for discussion. This could be followed up with requirements for 'additional information'. That is where the role of the Military ceases and that of the generalist commences with little further contribution from the Military. The resultant 'systemic' fault line that forms, rooted as it is in past misapprehensions, denies the decision-making process of a vibrant contribution by professionals with a high stakes and a lifetime involvement with those very issues.

There is in addition, a 'morale' aspect. Several mid-ranking Military officers feel the 'system' as being needlessly doubting their intentions and thereby their integrity and commitment to the nation. They have what they consider to be a legitimate claim to be integrated into the national development canvas and look forward to contributing with pride, not only in defence and security areas but across other areas of Government where their professional knowledge and experience can be put to good effect.

To revert to Lindsay Kohn with whose quote this Chapter commenced, his view is that:

> *'The State must, as a matter of ongoing policy, clearly and precisely specify the role of the Military. Certain uniformed leaders can and should be consulted in this process as the mission of the military changes to suit new conditions.... Furthermore, every effort must be made to limit the military to external defence so that it functions as representatives of the whole society acting in the best interest of the entire nation. Military forces should be used for internal order only in dire emergency so that they see themselves, and are seen, as the guardians and not the oppressors of the population; the organs of courts, police, militia, or border/security guards should keep order and execute the laws'.*

This, Lindsay Kohn emphasises, is on a condition that *'the military cannot define its own function or purpose'*.[4]

NOTES

1. Cohn, Lindsay, 'The Evolution of the Civil–Military "Gap" Debate' (Duke University 1999) @ http://tiss-nc.org/wp-content/uploads/2015/01/Cohn_Evolution-of-Gap-Debate-1999.pdf
2. Desch, Michael C., *Civilian Control of the Military–The Changing Security Environment*, John Hopkins University Press, 1999, p. 6.
3. Schiff, Rebecca L., 'Civil–Military Relations Reconsidered: A Theory of Concordance' (SAGE @ https://www.researchgate.net/publication/249775531_Civil-Military_Relations_Reconsidered_ A_Theory_of_Concordance
4. Cohn, Lindsay, 'The Evolution of the Civil–Military "Gap" Debate' (Duke University, 1999) @ http://tiss-nc.org/wp-content/uploads/2015/01/Cohn_Evolution-of-Gap-Debate-1999.pdf

CHAPTER 2

HISTORICAL PERSPECTIVE

CIVIL–MILITARY RELATIONS OVER THE AGES

The Mauryan Period

As often mentioned by Military officers, in primitive societies and well into the early ages, the 'King' was also the 'Commander in Chief', both responsibilities resting in the same person. It was the King alone who decided all 'policy' issues from going to battle or assigning roles to individuals. There would no doubt have been 'elders' and 'counsellors' who contributed to the decision making. But it was the Supreme Authority who made the decisions based upon all he knew from both the 'Civil' and 'Military' sides that vested in the King and him alone.

With progress of time, these two roles split with a King generally remaining as the supreme authority of both 'Civil' and Military sides but devolving authority of commanding the Military upon a Commander-in-Chief. Megasthenes '*Indica*' mentions that in the Mauryan State, *the fifth caste is the Military. It is well organised and equipped for war, holds the second place in point of numbers, and gives itself up to idleness and amusement in the times of peace. The entire force—men-at-arms, war-horses, war-elephants, and all-are maintained at the king's expense*' and that '*all power of the State was vested in the Emperor with the Commander-in-Chief being appointed by and functioned under the Emperor*'. Power vested in the 'Civil'

Emperor and the 'Military', under the Commander-in-Chief (C-in-C) was an instrument of State power to execute the directions of the Emperor.

Megasthenes places Councillors *in the Seventh and Controlling Caste.* These were men of high character, learning and wisdom who were advisors to the Emperor. It was their role to discuss and debate issues and situations and render advice to the Emperor. *Though the Military itself was placed in the 'Fifth' caste, the Commanders of the Military also hailed from this 'Seventh' caste.*

An important aspect of Mauryan administration was the 'Commissariat Board' that provided logistic support to the Military and managed accounts. This Board comprised entirely of civilians but their role had a direct impact on the effectiveness of the military and amounted to 'direct participation' of Civilians in the management of affairs of the Military.

Kautilya's *Arthashastra* advises the King to rule through Vision (*Prabhu Shakti*), Mission (*Mantra Shakti*) and Motivation *(Utsah Shakti).* He emphasises that an Army not given its due honours, its due salaries, and for whatever reasons low in morale, abandoned by its Commander cannot perform efficiently. There is, equally, the requirement to provide the Army with requisite resources and be properly equipped and reinforced to sustain its fighting prowess.

The Mughals: A Conjoint Administrative and Military Structure

The Mughal Government was essentially military in origin and retained a strong military character. The Emperor was the head of the Army and its Commander-in-Chief. Under Akbar all government officials were also enrolled in the Army and nominated as commanders of a specified number of horsemen. Mughal Forces consisted of the cavalry, infantry, artillery, elephants and the war-boats (there was no Mughal Navy). The cavalry was the most important wing and regarded as the 'flower' of the Army with the infantry being the largest wing, though very often ill paid and the artillery consisting of gunners and musketeers.

In this Mansabdari system of Akbar, civil and military personnel were organised in a system of ranks or *mansabs* based on the decimal system. *Mansabdars* were numerically graded from Commanders of 10 to 5000 troops or horsemen. *There was no 'contract' between the Emperor and individual troops. Instead there was complete subordination of the latter who were recruited, reported to and paid by the* Mansabdar *under who the troop or a horseman served.* The Mansabdars in turn were organised hierarchically each lesser under one higher with the senior most taking their directions from the Emperor. *The 'civil' and the 'military' were truly 'merged' with leading Mansabdars being military commanders as also councilors and government functionaries.*

The Evolution of Extant Control Mechanisms

Present day Civil–Military Relations and Higher Defence Management structures, however, derive from those during British Raj. The focus for this book hereafter is therefore on relations between the 'Civil' and the 'Military' during the time of British rule and in post-independence India.

The East India Company

Beginnings and the Presidency Armies: The origins of the Indian Army, the first of the modern day Defence Forces in the sequence of their induction, trace back to recruitment of guards for the protection of their several factories. By the beginning of the eighteenth century, there were three fortified positions at Calcutta (Fort William), Madras (Fort St George) and Bombay, which came to be the locations for the three 'Presidencies'. These Presidencies were independent of each other and reported separately to the East India Company Headquarters in London. Their Presidents were also the C-in-Cs of the respective Armies, with troops who were both European and Indian. These Armies functioned as independent forces to meet the requirements and objectives of their Presidencies.

A C-in-C for India Appointed: Such a state continued till 1748 when the Company appointed a single overall Commander-in-Chief for all its forces in India. Simultaneously, another decision was taken to permanently locate troops of the Regular British Army in India, and the first contingent of British troops arrived in 1754. With this, there came to be three categories of troops—the King's Troops, the Company's European Troops and its Indian Troops. In 1757, there was an initiative to reorganise troops of the three Armies into 'Battalions' in which Indian soldiers would serve under a nucleus of English Officers and English Non-Commissioned Officers (NCOs) instead of only under Indian NCOs as hitherto.

The Regulating Act of 1773: The first reform in the 'Higher Defence Management' of the Company's Forces in India, however, came in 1773 through the Regulating Act which created the post of 'Governor General' who was supported by a Council of four members to make 'rules, ordinances and regulations for the good order and civil government' of all the Company's territories. The C-in-C was one of these members of the Council. The Pitts India Act 1784 reduced the number of members of the Council to three but the C-in-C continued to be a member of the Council.

The 'Military Department' and 'Military Member': In 1786, a 'Military Department' was constituted with the responsibility to communicate directions and orders of the C-in-C to the three Presidential Armies and placed under a 'Military Member' who was also a member of the Governor General's Council. Whereas the C-in-C controlled operational matters, other matters relating to the three Presidency Armies were coordinated by the Military Member. *As the C-in-C at times personally led operations, which entailed his absence from the Headquarters for extended periods, the Military Member's presence on the Council assured continued advice on matters Military to the Governor General's Council.*

The Charter Act of 1793: The East India Company Act 1793, also known as the Charter Act of 1793 affirmed powers on the Governor-General's of over-ruling his council was perhaps the first time when the strands of 'Civil' and 'Military' so far closely interwoven, were segregated with the stipulation that *the Commander-in-Chief would no longer be an ex-officio regular member of the Council but could be nominated as an extraordinary member by the Directors.*

The Charter Act of 1833: Charter Act of 1833, also known as the Saint Helena Act 1833 or Government of India Act 1833, followed, which introduced two memberships, military and legal, into the Governor General's Council. The Act specifically laid down that 'the superintendence, direction and control of the whole civil and military government shall be and is invested in the Governor General-in-Council'. Accordingly, a Military Member was appointed in 1834.

This Military Member had the responsibility to provide 'expert advice' on military matters to the Governor General, which would lessen his burden on matters military as also to limit the C-in-C to executive duties of managing the Army. *The Military Member, during the period he held that office was not to hold any military command or be deployed on any military duties, which precluded his being a functional subordinate to the C-in-C.* This arrangement remained in force until 1861.

The "Barnes Episode": An incident of great significance took place in 1832, consequent to Lt Gen Edward Barnes being appointed C-in-C in India, which compelled the Company Directors to address, for the first time, the issue of primacy of the Civil Authority over the Military.

Lt Gen Barnes was no ordinary 'run of the mill' Military Officer. In the course of his chequered career, he served in the Staff of the Duke of Wellington, participated in the invasion of Martinique and the Battle of Vitoria, besides the Battle of Waterloo in which he was wounded. Significantly, he was appointed Acting Governor of Ceylon from 1st February 1820 to 2nd February 1822 and was Governor of Ceylon from 1824 to 1831. In the course of his tenure, he was instrumental for the building of the military road between Colombo and Kandy, and of many other lines of communication. He organised the conduct of the first census in Ceylon and introduced coffee cultivation based on the West Indian system.

In 1832, he was appointed C-in-C in India with the local rank of General. As C-in-C in India he was required to function under the then Governor General Lord William Bentinck. Gen Barnes could not accept a subordinate role requiring the matter being referred to the Secretary of State in London, who, however, ruled in favour of the Governor General.

General Barnes thereupon relinquished his Command. The episode brought closure to any doubts on which authority the Governor General and the C-in-C was prime.

Changes After 1857: After the events of 1857, there were a number of decisions which had implications for the civil–military balance of the future. In 1858, the Company's European troops were merged with the Imperial British Army. Some Units of Indian Troops were disbanded and others reorganised and amalgamated. Recruitment was restricted to 'martial races' and Units of the British Army toured India on duty akin to garrisons despatched to other Colonies.

Prior to 1861, British Officers belonged to regimental cadres, which were unable to absorb voids caused by officers being posted to civil appointments and to staff appointments at the Headquarters of various Armies. There were wide variations in the promotion prospects between different Regiments and no equality of promotion opportunity between officers of the same rank across regiments. This was resolved by placing the entire officer strength of each Presidential Army into three 'Presidency Staff Corps', which served as a common resource pool to meet both Regimental and Staff requirements.

In 1861, there came to be two members of the Governor General's Council who were concerned with work relating to the Military. The C-in-C was the executive head of the Military with command and executive responsibility but with no 'portfolio' in the Governor General's Council. It was the 'Military Member', also a Military officer and junior in rank to the Commander-in-Chief, who instead held the portfolio and had responsibility for administration. It was through the Military Member that the C-in-C referred all proposals requiring approvals and decisions of the Government. Glimpses of the roles the Ministry of Defence plays today are visible in the role of the Military Member post-1861, though some Military historians choose to give credit for this to the Charter Act of 1833.

Consolidation of the Military Accounts Department: In 1864, the Military Accounts Departments of the three Presidencies were merged into a single Military Accounts Department, which was placed under an

Accountant General, Military Department, who in turn functioned under the Military Member.

Army Organisation Commission and the Abolition of Presidency Armies: Lord Lytton, the Viceroy in 1879, appointed an 'Army Organisation Commission' with the aim of examining military expenditures and improving its functional efficiency. This Committee, inter alia, recommended the abolition of the Presidency Armies, a proposal not immediately implemented. However, the three Presidency Staff Corps were merged into a single 'Indian Staff Corps' thereby introducing a pan-India cadre of British Officers. The Presidency Armies were subsequently abolished with effect from 01 Apr 1895 giving place to a centrally administered Indian Army organised into four Commands, each under a General Officer Commanding-in-Chief (Lt Gen) who exercised delegated powers but subordinate to the Commander-in-Chief.

These initial four Commands were (a) The Punjab Command (including the North West Frontier); (b) The Bengal Command; (c) The Madras Command (including Burma); (d) The Bombay Command (including Sindh, Quetta and Aden). Hence, an "Indian Army" as such came into being only in 1895 after the abolition of the Presidency Armies and the abolition of the Indian Staff Corps and all its officers designated as 'Officers of the Indian Army'.

Administrative Control of the 'Indian Army': The overall responsibility for all aspects of governance in India rested with the Governor General-in-Council who was responsible to the Secretary of State for India and through him to the British Parliament. The Governor General's Council had two members concerned with matters of the Military. First was the C-in-C who was the Executive Head of the Army and the Marines and responsible for the organisation and efficiency of the Army, and the second was the 'Military Member' with responsibility for the administrative work of the Army, viz. Supply and Transport, Ordnance, Military Works and Military Finance Department (including preparing the Military Budget). **Importantly, his role was also to communicate orders of the Government to the executive head of the Army, i.e. the C-in-C.**

The 'Duality Debate' on the Role of the Military Member: An extract of the 'Report of the Army Organisation Committee' (1879) relating to the 'Position of the Commander-in-Chief as a member of the Supreme Government' reads as follows:

> *The position of the Executive Commander-in-Chief as a member of the Committee is, in the opinion of the majority, one without precedent in the organisation of any European government or army. It is contrary to one of the most essential salutary principles of sound administration....and the common instinct and experience of all administrations, whether representative or despotic, had everywhere rejected it.*
>
> *... It is the constant duty of the Commander-in-Chief to be urging on the Government the expenditure of money for the improvement of the Army, and it is to him that the officers and men of the army must look up to press their claims and state their requirements. It is the constant duty of the government of India, on the other hand, in the interests of the tax payers of India, to refuse demands for expenditure which they consider unreasonable or unnecessary or beyond the power of the country to bear. When the Commander-in-Chief has, as executive head of the army and as a subordinate of the Government of India, said all that he can to properly urge in support of his views, he has performed his duties as an advocate, and it should then rest with those responsible for the government of the country to determine how far they can reconcile it to their sense of duty to accede to his requests....*[1]

The Military Department's role was two-fold. It not only carried out its original work under its own authority, but also carried out examination of proposals received for consideration from the Army Headquarters and the Command Headquarters. The Military Department maintained its own record files on various proposals thereby building up reference compendiums of 'precedence' cases to guide future decision making.

The procedure for consideration of proposals entailed these being forwarded to the Military Department through the Controller of Military Accounts. These were examined and upon approval by the Military Member were forwarded to the Finance Department and after being approved there, submitted to the Governor General. In case of disagreement, the case was placed before the Executive Council. The decisions of the Executive Council, as also the proposals approved by the

Governor General in which both Departments had agreed, were forwarded in a despatch to the Secretary of State and implemented only after his consent. Hence, the effective final control over all major decisions of consequence rested finally with the Secretary of State in London.

Two Military Officials being present in the Executive Council was a clearly an anomalous arrangement considering that one of them was the C-in-C himself and the other an officer junior to him but bearing responsibility to scrutinise proposals forwarded by the C-in-C and of conveying to him orders of the Government on the proposals put up by the C-in-C. The proposals forwarded by the C-in-C for approval of the Governor General were, as per procedure, required to be routed through the Military Member. As a result, a layer consisting of relatively junior officers came to be formed who evaluated proposals forwarded with the approval of the C-in-C. The flaws and infirmities in such a system was obvious.

The exasperation and frustration in the Army, even at the level of the C-in-C, is obvious in the comments recorded in 1889 by the then C-in-C Lord Roberts that a '*fresh evil has been growing in the shape of excessive noting and criticism in the Military Department on purely military aspect of proposals which are submitted with the weight and authority of the C-in-C, whereby unnecessary delay is caused and the main issue is frequently obscured by a mass of irrelevant criticism. The evils of this arrangement are palpable. All the work involving reference between army Headquarters and the Military Member has to be done twice over. Neither the C-in-C nor the Military Member of the Council see the arguments on which the opinion of the other is based and the Viceroy is apt to see the side of the Military Department in every case*'.[2] This system, however, continued and remained in vogue till 1906. (Not much imagination is required to draw comparison with present-day procedures).

The Curzon-Kitchener Standoff

It was not long before matters expectedly came to a head. Lord Curzon a 'rising star' of the British Empire, was appointed Viceroy in 1899 and soon set upon reforming the military apparatus in India. Ironically, he chose Lord Horatio Kitchener, the then C-in-C in South Africa who had successfully led the British victory in the Boer War, to be the C-in-C in India.

Kitchener's View on the Role of the Army: Kitchener assumed charge as C-in-C in India in 1902 and soon commenced his own plans to reform the Indian Army. In Kitchener's view, the Indian Army needed to discard the 'mutiny syndrome' that clouded its functioning. According to him, the primary role of the Indian Army was to guard the frontiers to which end it was imperative that all Units be trained to be deployed wherever on the borders when the occasion arises. He found the decision-making apparatus to be unsatisfactory for operational effectiveness. Kitchener was convinced that 'the then existing system was faulty, inefficient and incapable of expansion necessary for a great war'. He expressed his frustration on the role of the Military Department by stating:

> *"No needed reform can be initiated, no useful measure can be adopted without being subject to vexatious and for the most part unnecessary criticism not merely as regards the financial effect of the proposal, but to its desirability or necessity from the purely military point of view"* and that *"in war, the system must break down and unless it is deliberately intended to court disaster through divided counsels and divided authority.... It (the Military Member in the Viceroy's Council) must be abolished".*[3]

The Military Member's Response: These charges against the Military Department were strongly refuted by the then Military Member Maj Gen Sir ER Ellis. He stated that *'far from being vexatious and dilatory, the Military Department had been responsible for initiating a number of important measures for the efficiency of the Army, such as the mobilisation scheme and creation of a field army, amalgamation of Presidency Armies and Departments, organisation of transport service, etc.'*

On the important point of principle that the C-in-C raised, Maj Gen Ellis stated:

> *The Army in India has but one head – the Governor General in Council, and the Military Member in the Council is the representative of the Governor General in Council in respect of all business which is not brought before the Council collectively. The Commander-in-Chief, on the other hand, commands the Army according to rule and practice.*[4]

Maj Gen Ellis quoted Sir George Chesney, who stated:

> *The Commander-in-Chief...naturally presses his proposal from the Military point of view, and very properly, for if he does not press it from the military side, no one else is likely to do so. The Military Member of Council, on the other hand, has to consider the business of Government as a whole, and Army expenditure in relation to the financial condition of Government, and to the general policy imposed on him by the Governor General in Council. How this affects a man's judgement may be seen from more than one distinguished instance. Lord Napier of Magdala when he was Military Member in Council had to look at things from a very different point of view, from that which he held as Commander-in-Chief.*

Further, he opined that '*the control and interference that the Commander-in-Chief resents is not that of the Military Member but that of the Government...*' and emphasised by stating, '*I maintain that effective criticism, not only from the financial point of view but from every aspect in which it affects other departments of the State, is not only vexatious but also necessary*' adding that '*Effective criticism must entail some delay*'.[5]

Curzon's Apprehensions: The Viceroy, Lord Curzon, however, viewed Kitchener's plan as being one that would obliterate Civilian Authority and having potential to rise the appointment of C-in-C to that of a Military Autocrat. Kitchener countered this as not true by emphasising that the ultimate authority in any case vested in the Secretary of State for India and thereby in Civilian hands. Curzon conveyed his dissent forcefully to the Secretary of State by writing to him that

> *We (the Government of India) dissent to the creation of an organisation to which no parallel exists, as far as we know, in any Army or any administration in the world, which would create a military despotism in surroundings where, in the absence of parliamentary or public control, it would be fraught with the maximum of danger, and which would, in our opinion, lead to a disastrous breakdown as soon as it was tested in practice.*[6]

The Ruling by the Secretary of State: The then Prime Minister, Author Balfour, a staunch Conservative, was of the view that the ultimate authority for the governance of India rested with the House of Commons and agreed with Kitchener's standpoint. As a consequence to acceptance of Kitchener's proposals, the following administrative decisions were brought into effect:

(a) The Military Member was dropped from the Viceroy's Council. The C-in-C thus remained as the only Military Officer on the Council.

(b) The Military Department became the 'Army Department' and placed under an Army Secretary of the rank of Major General. This Department was placed under the C-in-C.

(c) A General Staff Branch was created in the Army Headquarters which was headed by the Chief of General Staff who was the Senior Principal Staff Officer.

(d) A Department of Military Supplies was created under another Civilian member of the Viceroy's Council.

Creation of the Military Finance Department: A significant spin off from the abolition of the Military Member was that the Military Accounts Department, which functioned under the Military Member was replaced by the Military Finance Department and placed under the Finance Member of the Viceroy's Council. The Resolution authorising this change specified the following:

(a) The Military Finance Secretary and his establishment would be located in the same premises as the Army Department. The Military Finance Secretary would be in direct and regular personal communication with the C-in-C.

(b) The C-in-C would, where thought desirable, take the advice of the Military Finance Secretary on the financial aspect of any military question, before making a formal reference to the Finance Department through the Military Finance Branch.

(c) The Military Finance Secretary would be a member of any Consultative Committee which may be formed to consider matters relating to administration of the Army.

(d) The Military Finance Secretary would in no way be subordinate to Military Authorities and be responsible only to the Finance Member of the Viceroy's Council.

Curzon Resigns: Curzon's resignation as Viceroy of India was triggered by the non-acceptance of his recommendation for the appointment of the Member (Military Supplies). In the course of his controversy with Kitchener, Curzon had even proposed that the creation of a Military Supplies Member was a waste of public money, an argument that was to be vindicated a few years later when the post was abolished. Apart from this 'corrective', the arrangement conceptualised by Kitchener remained unchanged unto 1946 through two World Wars right up to 1946 when an Indian defence Minister from the 'Interim Government' assumed Office in 1946.

The Esher Committee Recommendations: After the Boer Wars and the public sentiment of these wars having been nearly lost, a 'War Office Reconstitution Committee' was set up to review the functioning of the British War Office. This Committee, headed by Lord Reginald Brett Esher made certain radical suggestions regarding the functioning of the War Office such as abolishing the appointment of C-in-C, setting up of the Army Council and for a Permanent Committee of Imperial Defence. It was the same Lord Esher who was deputed to visit India to examine the functioning of the Military in India. The terms of reference for the Esher Committee he headed included examination of the position of the C-in-C in his dual capacity as head of the Army and Member of the Executive Council. Two Indian members on the Committee—Sir KG Gupta, a leading lawyer and Sir Umar Hyat Khan, a prominent Landlord of the Punjab were members on the Esher Committee.

The Esher Committee was of the unanimous view that the C-in-C should continue to render military advice to the Government of India and that no other Military officer should be on the Executive Council alongside him. It also did not accept a proposal to have a civilian member of the Executive Council for the Army, or an Army Council with 'collective responsibilities' which, the Committee concluded were 'unsuitable to Indian conditions'.

The Esher Committee also considered but did not accept the merger of the Army Headquarters and the Army Department based on the UK pattern as the C-in-C was in any case the Head of both bodies. However, to integrate their functioning, it recommended setting up of a 'Military Council' to be headed by the C-in-C with the Chief of General Staff,

Adjutant General, Quarter Master General, Army Secretary and the Financial Advisor as members. It was unanimously suggested by the Committee that the right to offer military advice to the Government of India must be solely that of the C-in-C and there should be no other Military officer in the Executive Council. It also considered the aspect of a Civilian Member being appointed for the Army Department.

The Montague-Chelmsford Act (1919): Post acceptance of the Montague Chelmsford reforms, the Central legislative assembly could discuss Defence matters but could not vote on Defence demands. The C-in-C became an ex-officio member of the Central Legislative Assembly Council and the Army Secretary of the Central Legislative Assembly.

A Civilian comes to be appointed as Secretary of the Army Department: A significant recommendation of the Esher Committee having immense bodings for the future was in regard to the post of Army Secretary. *All Secretaries of the Government of India including the Army Secretary had to report directly to the Viceroy.* The Army Secretary being a serving Major General, the Committee felt could provide the Viceroy with an additional window for obtaining advice on Military matters. To obviate such contingency, it recommended the post of Army Secretary be held henceforth by a Civilian officer. This recommendation was accepted and officers from the Indian Civil Service were posted as the Army Secretary. This appointment was later to be re-designated and become the genesis for the present day appointment of Defence Secretary.

The 'Constitutional' Position on Responsibility for India's Defence: The ultimate responsibility for prescribing a defence policy relating to India lay with the British Government. Defence, as a subject was outside the purview of the Legislatures and the authority for control within India lay with the Governor General-in-Council and through him and the Secretary of State for India, the House of Commons.

In March 1921, the Legislative Assembly passed a resolution that the purpose of the Army in India was the defence of India against external aggression and maintenance of internal peace and tranquillity. This resolution went against the grain and spirit of the Esher Committee Report which was that the administration of India cannot be considered otherwise than part of the total Armed Forces of the Empire and for the military resources of India being developed in a manner suited to Imperial necessities. This resolution had been accepted by the Government of India with an assurance to equip and organise the Indian Army on the lines of the British Army. There was however an awareness that complete assimilation will not take place owing to financial and other reasons. In 1928, the Cabinet Committee on the Defence of India decided (in view of the looming threat of a Russian invasion on India) that the *Defence Policy would revolve on an attack by a great power upon India or upon the Empire through India' and the derived position was that everything done in the defence of India was also done for the defence of the Empire and everything done in the defence of the Empire, whether in India or elsewhere, is also done in the defence of India.*

The Simon Commission Report and the demand for democratic control of the Army: The Simon Commission had met with considerable resentment from the Indians for their undemocratic policies. The Report of the Simon Commission had stated that '*India and Britain are so related that Indian defence cannot, now or in any future which is within sight, be regarded as a matter of purely Indian concern. The control and direction of such an army must rest in the hands of agents of the Imperial Government*'. The Congress, in response to the Simon Commission Report published the 'Nehru Report' that demanded 'full responsible government and dominion status for India'. Sir Tej Bahadur Sapru who drafted the portion of the Report dealing with Military matters had stressed the need for democratic control over the Army by stating '*We believe that the representation of the Army in the Legislature by a responsible Minister, who will, in actual administration, no doubt be guided by expert advice, is bound to lead to the establishment of more intimate relations between the Army and the Legislature...*'.[7]

The Nehru Report also recommended accelerating the rate of '*Indianisation* of the Armed Forces', the then rate of which it opined would take 'at least a century before the Army is really *Indianised*'. Another recommendation of the Committee was for defence expenditure to be sanctioned by a vote of the House of Representatives.

Recommendations following the First Round Table Conference 1931: Mahatma Gandhi's Civil Disobedience Movement had placed the British Government under pressure to grant additional concessions to meet Indian aspirations. During the first Round Table Conference, held in London, the government appointed a Sub-Committee on Defence (Sub Committee VII) whose members included luminaries such as Srinivasa Sastri, Tej Bahadur Sapru, Sir Phiroze Sethna, M.R. Jayakar, Dr B.S. Moonje and M.A. Jinnah. The Report of this Committee included a resolution that "with the development of the new political structure in India, the Defence of India must, to an increasing extent, be the concern of the Indian people and not of the British Government alone". It further stated that '*immediate steps be taken to increase substantially the rate of Indianisation in the Indian Army to make it commensurate with the main object in view, having regard to all relevant considerations, such as the maintenance of the requisite standard of efficiency*'. The recommendation of this Sub Committee that was to have a significant direct impact was for the setting up of a military training college in India 'at the earliest moment' and which eventually led to the institution of the Indian Military Academy.

The Government of India Act, 1935

The Act did not make any substantial changes to the mechanism for control of the military organisation. The maintenance of the Armed Forces continued to be an exclusive Federal subject with Section 11(1) of the Act empowering the Governor General to discharge functions in regard to Defence and Ecclesiastical Affairs 'in his discretion'.

A C-in-C was to be appointed under a Royal warrant and while Section 9(1) provided for a Council of Ministers to advise the Governor General in exercise of his functions, except for those subjects (including Defence) which he was to discharge at his discretion. For such subjects, the Governor General could appoint not more than three Cousellors to advise him. As the functions of the C-in-C were not clearly specified, an ambiguity arose as to his position vis-à-vis the Counsellors. However, as the proposed Federal Government did not materialise, the position of the C-in-C remained as stipulated in the earlier Government of India

Act 1919. In any case, as per the warrant of Precedence, the C-in-C ranked only next to the Governor General along with the Governors of Bengal, Bombay and Madras and Governors of Provinces within their States.

CONTROL MECHANISM DURING TRANSITION TO INDEPENDENCE

Interim Government and Appointment of an Indian 'Defence Member' (1946)

With the formation of an Interim Government in India on 02 September 1946, an Indian, Sardar Baldev Singh, was appointed as the Defence Minister on 19 September 1946. *With this appointment, a tectonic shift took place in the position of the C-in-C who, from his pre-eminent position as the sole supremo of the Military in India, now was de facto the No 2 in the Government hierarchy. He ceased to be an Extraordinary member of the Executive Council remaining as the Executive Head of the three Defence Services and an Adviser to the Defence Minister.*

Defence Minister's Committee

A Defence Member's Committee was set up under the Chairmanship of the Defence Member with the C-in-C, the Defence Secretary and the Financial Adviser as members with the Secretary to the C-in-C's Committee as its Secretary. The C-in-C's Committee, however, continued to also exist and dealt with 'Inter-Service' matters and in drawing up policy on Defence matters. Matters that came before the C-in-C's Committee were initially considered by the Chiefs of Staff Committee.

It is pertinent that a proposal for a Cabinet Committee on Defence in the Interim Government could not be implemented as the Muslim League, which also joined the Government had NOT accepted the concept of 'joint responsibility' of the Cabinet.

Preserving Sanctity of Command and Authority of the C-in-C

A piquant situation emerged as it was necessary to maintain in the hearts and minds of soldiers the dignity and primacy of command of the Armed

Forces under the C-in-C under whom they served. There is an interesting episode often mentioned in the Army Headquarters about the case of soldier whose appeal against a sentence by a Court Martial had came up before the new Defence Minister in his capacity as the final appellate authority after the C-in-C had turned down an earlier plea. Sardar Baldev Singh, the Defence Minister was inclined to grant the appeal. Field Marshal Auchinleck, the C-in-C in deference to the constitutional position of the Defence Minister preferred to revise his own earlier orders himself and sought permission to do so that his order on the case would remain as the final one. This oft-mentioned episode emphasises the importance of maintaining the sanctity of a Commander's directions in the eyes of his force. This is everyone's' concern to maintain and preserve as eventually, it is this sanctity besides faith and trust, that underlies the efficacy of the command and control mechanism of the Armed Forces.

The Supreme Commander for Armed Forces: Reconstitution of the Armed Forces and Control of the Armed Forces during Reconstitution

With the announcement of transfer of power to the two dominions of India and Pakistan, it was also announced that the Commander-in-Chief would be appointed as the Supreme Commander for both dominions with responsibility for the reconstitution of the Armed forces of both. A Cabinet decision was taken on 06 June 1947 to set up a Committee under the Viceroy to work out the mechanisms for implementing partition. It was decided that there would be two members of the Congress and the Muslim League who would, through a special 'Steering Committee' of two officials, 'conduct and coordinate detailed investigations at the expert level on various problems arising from the partition of the country'. There were ten expert committees who would cover various Departments of the Government of India. The 'Armed Forces Reorganisation Committee' was in fact 'Committee No X' of these Expert Committees.

General Claude Auchinleck, who became the Commander-in-Chief in 1943, who was an Indian Army officer and a realist could anticipate the eventual political reality of transfer of power and emphasised the need for rapid Indianisation of the Armed Forces. In March 1945, Gen

Auchinleck recommended that in future only Indians should be granted permanent commissions in the Army. This recommendation was accepted resulting in a Government announcement made on 22 October 1945, as follows:

> *The grant of permanent commissions in the Royal Indian Navy and the Indian Army will, in future, be restricted to Indians and to other persons domiciled in India who are subjects of His Majesty's or of a Prince or Chief in India. The recruitment of officers to the Royal Indian Air Force is already subject to this restriction ... it will be generally recognised that the three Indian Services will still require a quota of British officers until such time as there is an adequate supply of qualified Indian officers... The quota of seconded or attached British officers of the three Indian Services will be systematically and progressively reduced as Indian officers become available.*[8]

> The Interim Government assumed power on 02 September 1946, and Jawaharlal Nehru as Vice President of the Viceroy's Executive Council conveyed to the C-in-C that '*one of (their) first tasks, as a national Government based on popular approval, is to attempt to transform the whole background of the Indian Army and make it feel that it is a national army of India. It was impossible for this to be done in the past because the whole conception of the Indian Army was different and the average soldier fought for more in terms of an external allegiance than for allegiance to his own country*, and emphasised that '*it is equally necessary to make the Indian public feel that the army is theirs and is not some kind of hostile force imposed on them. They should be proud of their army*'. On his part, the C-in-C Gen Auchinleck communicated to all Army Commanders that '*It has been decided, and in my opinion inevitably decreed, that we – the British officers – are to go*'.

Armed Forces Nationalisation Committee

On 30 November 1946 an Armed Forces Nationalisation Committee was appointed with Sir Gopalaswamy Ayyangar as its Chairman. The Terms of Reference of the Committee mentioned the stated purpose of its formation being '*to nationalise the armed forces of India, namely the Indian Navy, the Indian Army and the Indian Air Force and all ancillary services, both officers and men, within the shortest possible time, with due regard to Indian national interests and reasonable efficiency ....*'[9]

The Committee envisaged a two-stage programme of Indianisation—the first ending in January 1947 and the second in January 1951. It did not, however, provide for a comprehensive Indianisation but recommended a phased approach. The Government too had generally argued against the rapid withdrawal of British officers. In his letter to the Defence Member of the Interim Government, Auchinleck wrote: '*I am firmly convinced that to attempt to achieve complete nationalisation of the Armed Forces, and especially of the Indian Army, by June 1948 is to run a very grave risk of their disintegration and disruption.*' Pundit HN Kunzru moved a Resolution in the Council of States for a time limit being fixed for the 'nationalisation' of the Armed Forces. The C-in-C, Gen Auchinleck, had argued against the resolution being adopted on grounds that it would be 'highly dangerous' and 'most undesirable'. The reason for this was that till March 1947 Auchinleck and most senior British officers were working on the assumption that division of the country would not entail bifurcation of the Armed Forces and that a substantial number of British officers would be retained in the undivided Armed Forces, which would have ensured Britain's control over the defence and foreign policy of both successor states. *In April 1947 however, the Government accepted 'in principle' that partition of the country would also involve the division of the Armed Forces.* The issue of 'nationalisation' of the Armed Forces thereafter lost its relevance and though the Nationalisation Committee submitted its report in May 1947, in view of the changed political circumstances, its report was not made public.

There is an interesting observation of Gen Auchinleck meriting being quoted that "*...the Indian has always thought, rightly or wrongly, that we never intended the scheme to succeed and expected it to fail. Colour was lent to this view by the way in which each new step forward had to be wrested from us, instead of being freely given. Now that we have given a lot we get no credit because there was little grace in our giving*".[10] The underlying truth revealed is that the entry of Indians into the officer ranks was perceived as a threat to the reliability of the Armed Forces as a tool of British imperialism.

It is to the credit and maturity of the then Indian political leadership that there was no attempt on their part to subvert the Armed Forces.

Mahatma Gandhi's nationalist non-violent movement kept the Armed Forces out of its purview, his mature views being best expressed in his words: '*I do not want them to be disloyal to the present Government in whose power they are, for if they are disloyal to the present Government today, by the same token they may be disloyal to the national government tomorrow*'.[11]

On 15 August 1947, Sardar Baldev Singh, Defence Minister in the earlier Interim Cabinet was appointed Independent India's first Defence Minister. Simultaneously, the single C-in-C for the Defence Forces ceased to exist and was replaced by three different Commanders-in-Chief for the Army, Navy and Air Force.

NOTES

1. Report of the Army Organisation Committee 1879.
2. Venkateswaran, A. L., *Defence Organisation in India*, Publications Division, 1967, p. 7.
3. Ibid., p. 8.
4. Ibid.
5. Ibid.
6. 'Historical Overview', *Review of the Management of Defence*, Ministry of Defence, 2000, p. 15.
7. The Nehru Report of 28-30 August, 1928 (Memorandum proposing a new dominion status constitution for India prepared by a committee of the All Parties Conference chaired by Motilal Nehru signed by Motilal Nehru, Ali Imam, Tej Bahadur Sapru, M.-S. Aney, Mangal Singh, Shuaib Qureshi, Subhas Chandra Bose, and G.R. Pradhan.)
8. Sapru Committee Report, 1945, App. XVII.
9. Terms of Reference Gopalaswamy Aiyyangar Committee, Committee for the Indianisation of Army.
10. Sharpe, Andrew, 'The Indianisation of the Indian Army', *History Today*, 36(3), 1986.
11. 'The Harijan', 10 March 1947 (From The Collected Works of Mahatma Gandhi, Vol. VII).

CHAPTER 3

POST-INDEPENDENCE DEVELOPMENTS

OVERVIEW

The post-independence Defence Policy was a tectonic shift from the past. The Indian Armed Forces were now no longer a 'theatre command' of the British Empire. Their primary role now had altered fundamentally from being an element of the defence policy of Imperial Britain to that of ensuring the security of Independent India. The need now was to assess threats the new nation India faced and to secure it against them. This had to be done against competing requirements for funds to fulfil social objectives of a new nation. Decisions required to be taken by the Cabinet concerned core defence-related issues, such as what the strengths of the nation's Armed Forces should be, how they should be organised, the purpose for which they would be deployed, long-term planning for their growth and development, the resources to be allocated for the purpose, etc.

During the days of the Raj, Higher Defence Management had been an exclusive purview of the British. The senior most Indian Military officers at the time of Independence were all relatively junior in age and service with limited experience and exposure in policy formulation. There were also very few Civil servants at that time with adequate experience on Defence matters. Hence, an all-round 'experience and expertise void' existed on both sides. It is in this backdrop that the evolution of mechanisms for control of the Armed Forces have to be examined.

DEFENCE COMMITTEE OF THE CABINET 1947

The first 'Higher Defence Control' organisation of Independent India was the constitution of the Defence Committee of the Cabinet (DCC) on 30 September 1947. The DCC was chaired by the Prime Minister (also at the time the External Affairs Minister) with the Deputy Prime Minister (Home Minister), the Finance Minister and Defence Minister as its members. Interestingly, the Heads of the three Armed Forces were to be in attendance in all meetings of the Defence Committee of the Cabinet to provide on-the-spot clarifications and appreciation. Likewise, the Defence Secretary and the Financial Adviser (Defence) were also to be present to provide clarifications on aspects of administrative and financial aspects.

The constitution of this Defence Committee was one amongst a series of structures for higher defence management conceived by Lord Hastings Lionel Ismay, the Chief of Staff to the Viceroy Lord Mountbatten. It is worthwhile to know of the credentials of this tall military personality as a backdrop to understanding his recommendations.

LORD ISMAY : AN OUTSTANDING OFFICER WITH AN EXCEPTIONAL CAREER

General Hastings Lionel "Pug" Ismay, was a British Indian Army officer and diplomat with unique experience of a prolonged association with higher defence structures in England. Commissioned into the 21st Prince Albert Victor's Own Cavalry, a Regiment of the Indian Army. He saw action in Afghanistan and Somalia before being appointed Assistant Secretary of the Committee of Imperial Defence. He thereafter was Military Secretary to Lord Willingdon, the Viceroy of India before returning as Deputy Secretary to the Committee of Imperial Defence.

In August 1938, Gen Ismay was appointed as Secretary of the Committee of Imperial Defence. In May 1940, when Winston Churchill became Prime Minister of the United Kingdom, he was appointed Chief

Military Assistant and Staff Officer to the Prime Minister. *In this capacity he served as the principal link between Churchill and the Chiefs of Staff Committee. Churchill in fact gave Ismay additional responsibility of even serving on the Chiefs of Staff Committee.* After the War, Ismay worked with a Committee to draft the Statement Relating to Defence which formed the basis of reforms, *earning him recognition for being the 'Chief Architect' of the post-war Ministry of Defence.* After his retirement from the Army, Lord Ismay accepted becoming Chief of Staff to Lord Louis Mountbatten, the Viceroy of India. With these credentials, Lord Ismay was indeed uniquely placed to render apt advice on how the higher defence management of the fledgling new nation should be organised.

PREVAILING SITUATION AT THE TIME LORD ISMAY'S PROPOSALS WERE DRAWN UP

It is pertinent to understand Lord Ismay's recommendations in the light of the prevailing circumstances of the time. This is imperative *as many old guards of the military have expressed a view that Ismay, though a military man had 'let them down'.*

Prior to Independence, the C-in-C had been the sole Commander for all three Forces. *A major decision already implemented was to have three separate Cs-in-C for each of the Services with their own respective Headquarters and dealing directly with the Defence Minister.* The other was the role of the Defence Secretary, who headed the Defence Ministry. This has been succinctly summarised by none other than HM Patel while delivering the Annual Kale Memorial Lecture in 1963 on "The Defence of India". HM Patel stated that:

> *while the Government was convinced of the undoubted importance of allowing the three services to developing its own way in matters which are distinctly its own, it was no less convinced that the necessary separation should not be pushed too far, for matters in which common organisation was possible could obviously be dealt with efficiency and economy if so organised, and what is more important would in the process assist in building up a feeling of the essential oneness of the defence organisation.*[1]

Further, *there is another aspect of 'leadership voids' within the Armed Forces.* World War II and post-partition reconstitution of the Armed Forces, had resulted in rapid promotions and advancements to higher command positions. Gen KM Cariappa was only forty-eight years of age at the time of his appointment as C-in-C on 15 January 1949. Two years prior, in 1947, he was a Brigadier. Air Marshal Subroto Mukherjee was then an Air Commodore and Naval Chiefs-to-be Katari and BS Soman were both in the rank of Captain (IN). Such 'juniority' and lack of experience would need to be taken into account while formulating Command and Control Structures for Independent India's Armed Forces.

This concern over lack of experience was reinforced by some of the views held by the prospective future military leadership. Inder Malhotra, in an article titled 'Khaki vs Khadi', featuring in the *Indian Express* of 17 October 2008, writes that 'In the midst of intense negotiations over this issue, on May 9, 1947, Brigadier (later the first Indian Commander-in-Chief of the Indian Army) K.M. Cariappa called on Mountbatten's chief of staff, Lord Ismay, to suggest that the power be transferred to the Indian Army with either Nehru or Jinnah as the Commander-in-Chief'. Taken aback by this 'amazing' and 'highly dangerous' proposal, Ismay, himself a distinguished General, remonstrated with Cariappa and reported the conversation to the Viceroy, saying: '*It is hard to know whether Cariappa ... was ingenuous and ignorant or ingenuous and dangerous*'.[2] The Home Minister, *Sardar Patel, too had apprehensions of the close links that Gen KM Cariappa had with the Pakistan Army and his 'inappropriate contacts' with some of its officers.*

LORD ISMAY'S PROPOSALS

Besides the Cabinet Committee on Defence (which was one amongst such Committees of the Cabinet including the Economics Committee, the Foreign Affairs Committee), Lord Ismay went on to recommend a set of subordinate structures which would not only support the Cabinet Committee on Defence but also provide a robust graded structure for coordinated decision making at various levels.

Defence Minister's Committee

A Defence Minister's Committee with the Defence Minister as Chairman, the C-in-C, Defence Secretary and the Financial Adviser as members had been set up during the Interim Government in 1946. This Committee was reconstituted to include the Cs-in-C of all three Services. It examined papers and proposals required to be submitted to the Defence Committee of the Cabinet and decided on such matters which concerned all three or at least two of the three Services but did not merit decision at the level of the Defence Committee of the Cabinet.

Defence Secretary's Committees

In 1948, there were separate Committees formed under the Chairmanship of the Defence Secretary for each of the three Services with the concerned Service Chief, Financial adviser and the Joint Secretary concerned with the Service as members. These Committees considered Administrative and Policy matters concerning the respective Service. They functioned until 1949 whereafter they were converted to the Defence Minister's Committees for the Army, Navy and the Air Force with the Defence Minister as Chairman and the concerned Service Chief, Defence Secretary and Financial Adviser as members.

The Chiefs of Staff Committee

The Chiefs of Staff Committee, consisting of the three Service Chiefs was the next level Committee set up under Lord Ismay's proposals comprising of the three Service Chiefs. The Chiefs collectively being the professional advisers to the Committee, this Committee was of immense importance and had the responsibility to prepare Military plans and advise the Government on all operational matters and military matters in general. The COSC also became a crucial forum for coordination between the three services. There was, however, no separate Chairman for the COSC and the mantle of Chairmanship came upon the Chief who had been longest serving on the Committee.

The seeds of what has become a contentious issue which dominates inter-services coordination and planning in the present day were in fact sown at this stage. In terms of Command and control of the three Defence Services, each Service Chief was responsible to the Government for all matters concerning his own service. At that time, when the Cs-in-C of the Air Force and the Navy were of the rank of Vice Admiral and Air Marshal respectively, an Army Chief with the rank of full general had chosen, in the interests of inter-services camaraderie to be a member of a Committee chaired by a longer serving Chief of a sister service notwithstanding his not of equivalent rank. *This has often been quoted by bureaucrats to question the intransigence of Service Chiefs to attend meetings called for by the Defence Secretary which, if agreed, would contribute substantially to resolving functional issues.*

Subordinate Committees

There were other 'Inter-Services' Committees also set up such as the Joint Planning Committee, Joint Training Committee (JTC), Joint Intelligence Committee (JIC), Inter-Services Equipment Policy Committee (ISEPC) and the Medical Services Advisory Committee (MSAC). In addition were the Principal Personnel Officers Committee and the Principal Supply Officers Committee which were differently composed in that, apart from the concerned PSOs of the three Services Headquarters, they also had as Members representatives of the Ministry of Defence and Finance (Defence). The arrangement was to be that if a proposal was unanimously accepted by either of these Committees, it did not require to be scrutinised in the Ministry so that procedural and administrative delays could be cut down. However, these Committees did not prove very effective. The Ministry of Defence had proposed to even wind up the PPOC and PSOC sometime during 1976 to which the Services Headquarters had strongly objected. The Committees continued but their contributions remained peripheral.

In 1965, the JIC was removed from the ambit of the Military Wing and charted a growth trajectory of its own.

The 'Military Wing' of the Cabinet Secretariat

A separate 'Military Wing' was set up in the Cabinet Secretariat in October 1947 to function under a Deputy Secretary (Military) as its head. The incumbent for this appointment was a Services officer of the rank of Brigadier and the post was held in rotation by the three Services. The administrative control over the Military Wing was of the Cabinet Secretary. *Secretariat support for all Inter-Services Committees was to be provided by the Military Wing of the Cabinet Secretariat, which thereby provided a window for the formal involvement of Services personnel in decision making.*

Access of Services Chiefs to the Defence Committee of the Cabinet

Lord Ismay's proposals included a provision for the Service Chiefs having a 'direct access' to the Defence Committee of the Cabinet 'if necessary through the Defence Minister's Committee'.

The then Defence Secretary, Shri HM Patel strongly objected to this recommendation, perhaps because all three Service Cs-in-C at the time were British officers.[3] The Defence Secretary's objections were accepted by the Defence Minister's Committee on 20 December 1947, thereafter Service Chiefs had access only to the Defence Minister and only through him to the Defence Committee of the Cabinet. This was one more in a series of measures that impacted the status of the Services Chiefs.

The Ministry of Defence and its new Role

The 'Defence Department' had been a 'sheltered Department' throughout the days of the Raj. It was not under the purview of the Legislature and its accounts were not voted. Though the Secretary of the Defence Department had been a Civilian ICS Officer since 1921 and most of its officers in fact had been from the ICS, they were overwhelmingly British officers. It was only in 1938 that an Indian Officer was posted to the Defence Department as an Under Secretary with another Indian ICS Officer appointed Additional Secretary in 1941. In 1942 for the first time that an Indian ICS Officer Chandulal Trivedi was appointed as Secretary of the Defence Department and held the post till 1946. ADF Dundall, a British ICS Officer who succeeded him, however, relinquished it the next year, having opted for Pakistan.

Likewise, a number of Muslim Officers in the Department had also opted for Pakistan creating a very large experience void in the administrative capabilities of the Defence Department as there were very few Indian Officers with any previous experience in dealing with matters of the Department. There were some officers who gained some experience by virtue of association with the partition of the Armed Forces amongst who were HM Patel and BB Ghosh, who were appointed Defence Secretary and Joint Secretary respectively. Both these Officers were to play a crucial and decisive role in not only shaping the manner in which the Ministry of Defence carried out its functions as also setting the future course for a functional relationship between the Defence Ministry and the Services Headquarters.

In the Military Finance Department, however, the situation was less critical. An Indian Officer had been appointed as Military Accountant General and Additional Financial Adviser for the first time as far back as 1919. Thereafter several Indian Officers held various appointments of Deputy and Assistant Financial Advisers and at the time of partition, a large number of the officers of the Department were Indians. *At the time of abolition of the Military Department the responsibility for scrutiny of Military expenditures largely came onto the shoulders of the Military Accounts Department and its officers came to have a close understanding of the functioning of the Military. This experience enabled the Department to provide guidance not only to the Ministry of Defence but also to the Services Headquarters during the initial post-Independence days.*

The C-in-C, being Supreme Commander of all three Services during British rule, no proposal from any of the Services Headquarters would reach the Defence Department without his approval. The C-in-C also coordinated the operational functioning of the three Services. With each Service now having its own C-in-C, the onus of coordinating and integrating the functions of the three Services also came to rest with the Defence Department.

With effect from 29 August 1947, all Departments of the Government of India were designated as Ministries and the Defence Department hence became the Ministry of Defence and the Military Finance Department as Ministry of Finance (Defence).

The Ministry of Finance (Defence)

The Ministry of Finance (Defence), headed by the Financial Adviser was responsible to the Finance Minister in the post-independence period on matters of budgeting and expenditure of the Defence Budget. The Financial Adviser is not just responsible for the preparation of the Defence Services Estimates. As per the recommendations of the Esher Committee, a Deputy Financial Adviser was attached to each major Branch of the Army Headquarters, an arrangement later expanded to cover the Naval and Air Headquarters, the Ordnance Factories and the Pension Departments. A Deputy Financial Adviser each was included onto the Principal Personnel Officers' Committee and the Principal Supply Officers' Committee.

The Services Headquarters come to be 'Attached Offices'

Perhaps the most significant step in the process of 'diluting' the position of the Armed Forces took place in 1952 with the issuance of the "Organisation, Functions, Powers and Procedure of Defence Headquarters, 1952". The decision to issue these Procedures was taken without any interface between the Chiefs of Staff and the Political authority. *This decision ensured that the Services Headquarters are not part of the Departmental structure of the Ministry of Defence but only 'Attached Offices' to the Department of Defence. 'Attached Offices' are generally responsible for providing executive direction required in the implementation of the policies laid down by the Department to which they are attached. They also serve as the repository of technical information and advise the Department on technical aspects of questions dealt by them.*

An aspect that caused some concern was not just that a decision of such magnitude had been routinely taken. It was equally, the manner in which it was taken. The then Cs-in-C were aware of such a proposal being under consideration. On 27 May 1952, the Defence Secretary, HM Patel informed Gen KM Cariappa Chairman Chiefs of Staff Committee of the proposal to designate the Services Headquarters as Attached Offices and sought his response within 20 days. After hectic consultations with the two other Cs-in-C, Gen Cariappa wrote back to the Defence Secretary on 13 June 1952 that the Services Chiefs had strong reservations on the intended changes and that the issue should be discussed in detail. No discussion took place and requests from Gen Cariappa's office seeking early scheduling of a discussion were ignored until, on

07 July, the Cabinet Secretariat notified Gen Cariappa of Government's approval to the proposal.

There was considerable debate on why such a proposal had been mooted and whether there was need at all to review the then existing working arrangement between the Ministry of Defence and the Service Headquarters. The common view expressed from the Services side is that the proposal emanated from a fear in the minds of the political leadership on possible misadventures especially in the light of the Junta had taken control over Pakistan, a fear they think was fuelled deliberately by the bureaucracy. The Bureaucrat's response to this is stoic. We are now in a democracy and it is the sole prerogative of the Government to determine what place and the role each organisation, including the Military, must assume in the body politic. The decision did not impinge in any way on the authority of the Chiefs as there were no amendments to the Acts that diluted the force of Command and Control over their respective Services.

Implications

The major implication of accepting the proposal is that the Ministry of Defence acquired the authority to make policy on all defence matters and strengthen their hold on virtually all aspects of administration and functioning of the Services Headquarters and through them, the Defence Services. The Services Headquarters as 'Attached Offices' had their responsibility now restricted to 'executing' the implementation of policies laid down by the Government besides serving, in terms of the Manual on Office Procedure as 'the repository of technical information and advise the Government on technical aspects of questions dealt with by them'.

Change in Designation of the Cs-in-C

The Supreme command of the Indian Armed Forces is vested in the President, although effective executive power and responsibility for National Defence resides with the Cabinet, headed by the Prime Minister and discharged through the Ministry of Defence, which is headed by the Minister of Defence. It is the function of the Ministry of Defence to draw up the requisite policy framework and ensure the provision of resources and wherewithal to the Armed Forces to enable them to discharge their responsibilities.

With effect from 15 August 1947, the appointment of 'C-in-C for the Armed Forces in India' ceased to exist and each of the three Services came to be headed by its own C-in-C. In 1955, the appointments of the three Services Chiefs were re-designated as the 'Chief of the Army Staff' (General), the 'Chief of the Naval Staff' (Vice-Admiral) and the 'Chief of the Air Staff' (Air Marshal). The Chief of the Air Staff was raised to the rank of Air Chief Marshal in 1965 and the Chief of the Naval Staff rose to the rank of Admiral in 1968. The title 'Commander-in-Chief' carried with it the heritage of a position of exceptional authority and aura. After Independence, all three Service Chiefs had assumed the title 'Commander-in-Chief' of their respective Services. The Constitution of India, which came into force on 26 January 1950, stipulated and the President of India was also the Commander-in-Chief of the Armed Forces. There was indeed a 'clash of nomenclatures' requiring resolution. The announcement made in Parliament by the then Prime Minister Jawaharlal Nehru, quoted below, elucidates the reasons for such re-designation:

> *It would be better if in future the designation of the Commander-in-Chief should be dropped and they should be called the Chiefs of Staff... It is proposed that the Heads of the Services in future be called Chief of Army Staff, Chief of the Naval Staff and Chief of the Air Staff, and in the course of a few days, orders to this effect will be issued. In some countries they do not have these Commanders-in-Chief in this manner, in fact in most countries they have some kind of Defence Councils...No doubt it may be desirable for us also to form these Councils...We are going into this matter and hope gradually to develop these Councils.*[4]

The issue before the Chiefs of Staff now was whether they continue to be the operational Commanders of their respective Forces or be Chiefs of Staff and delegate Operational responsibility to Commanders. On their part they chose to be separate 'juridical entities' under the Army, Navy and Air Force Acts as applicable and have a legal status outside the Government.

The Councils, in the spirit of Nehru's statement to Parliament never took shape. But the reason for this was the opposition and stiff resistance from the Service Chiefs themselves. The proposed Councils, to be chaired by the Defence Minister would inter alia have as members the Service Chiefs but also select PSOs from respective Headquarters. It was against the grain of service ethos for a subordinate being allowed freedom to express an opinion contrary to that of his superior especially when the latter was the operational commander of the service.

The Estimates Committee of Parliament 1958

A functional appraisal of the Defence Organisation was carried out for the first time in 1958, after a period of ten years since Independence by the Estimates Committee of Parliament headed by the late Shri Balwantrai Mehta. The Report submitted by this Committee on the 'Organisation of the Ministry of Defence and Services Headquarters' found that *'the existing system was inefficient, not making for economy or speedy decision making, ridden by considerable duplication with various segments functioning in a compartmentalised manner instead of moving jointly towards achieving common objectives'.*

Moreover, importantly, the Committee also observed the imbalance in the distribution of responsibility and authority between the Services Headquarters and the Ministry of Defence and recommended a comprehensive review of the existing powers and delegation of more power to the Services Headquarters. To this end, it recommended a 'Council' system as in the UK, the amalgamation of Finance and Accounts systems to bring about economy and efficiency and suggested the Railway Financial Administration System be studied for adoption to the Defence Organisation as a whole.

AoB and ToB Rules 1961

In 1961, the President of India, Dr Rajendra Prasad, issued over his own signatures the Allocation of Business Rules and the Transaction of Business Rules 1961. While the Allocation of Business Rules 1961 allocate the business of the Government among its different departments, which are assigned to the charge of the Ministers by the President on the advice of the Prime Minister, the Transaction of Business Rules 1961 seek to define the authority, responsibility and obligations of each department in the matter of disposal of business allotted to it.

Further, the Rules provide that the business allotted to a department will be disposed of by, or under the direction of, the Minister-in-Charge and also specify the cases or classes of cases to be submitted to the President, the Prime Minister, the Cabinet or its committees for prior approval and the circumstances in which the department primarily concerned with the business under disposal will have to consult other departments concerned and secure their concurrence before taking a final decision. There is no mention of the Service Headquarters or their Chiefs in these Rules or their Appendices. The eventual responsibility for the defence of India or any part thereof rests on the Defence Secretary.

The following defining terms mentioned in these Rules need to be carefully understood:[5]

A 'Department'

A 'Department', also called 'Secretariat', is defined/described as being 'responsible for the formulation of the policies of the Government within its sphere of responsibility and also for the execution and review of those policies'.

For the efficient disposal of business allotted to it, a department is divided into wings, divisions, branches and sections. A Department is normally headed by a Secretary to the Government of India who acts as the Administrative Head of the Department and Principal Adviser of the Minister on all matters of policy and Administration within the Department.

Where the volume of work in a department exceeds the manageable charge of a Secretary, one or more wings may be established with a Secretary/Special Secretary/Additional Secretary/Joint Secretary in charge of each wing. Such a functionary is normally vested with the maximum measure of independent functioning and responsibility in respect of the business falling within his wing subject, however, to the overall responsibility of the Secretary for the Administration of the Department as a whole.

The distribution of subjects among the departments is specified in the Second Schedule to these rules and 'includes all attached and subordinate offices or other organisations including Public Sector Undertakings concerned with its subjects and sub-rules (2), (3) and (4) of this rule'.

(b) An 'Attached Office'

Attached and Subordinate offices have the under mentioned role and functions:

(i) Where the execution of the policies of the Government requires decentralisation of executive action and/or direction, a department may have under it executive agencies called 'Attached' and 'Subordinate' offices.

(ii) Attached offices are generally responsible for providing executive direction required in implementation of the policies laid down by the department to which they are attached. They also serve as repository of technical information and advise the department on technical aspects of questions dealt with by them.

(iii) Subordinate offices generally function as field establishments or as agencies responsible for the detailed execution of the policies of Government. They function under the direction of an attached office, or where the volume of executive direction involved is not considerable, directly under a department. In the latter case, they assist the departments concerned in handling technical matters in their respective fields of specialisation.

The position of the Services Headquarters and through them, the Defence Services under these Rules is candidly clear. They had now been firmly notified as 'executive agencies' to carry out directions of the Defence Secretary whose task it is to draft and obtain approval from the Government and communicate these for implementation to the Defence Services. Hence any proposal for the Defence Services to be included in the 'Apex Structure' of the Government and its decision making apparatus, they (its Chiefs and functionaries), their role and specific responsibilities will require to be specifically incorporated into these rules.

NOTES

1. Kale Memorial Lectures, Gokhale Institute of Politics and Economics, Pune (1973).
2. 'Khaki vs Khadi' by Inder Malhotra *Indian Express* (New Delhi) 17 October 2008.
3. Gen KM Cariappa assumed the appointment of C-in-C only on 15 January 1949.
4. Lok Sabha proceedings 25 May 1955.
5. Extracted from The Government of India (Allocation of Business) Rules, 1961.

CHAPTER 4

PERSONALITY PLAY

There have been interesting instances that took place in the course of interface between Civilian Authority and the Military leadership, along with what is regarded in the Defence Services to be their being 'boxed in', the stature of their Chiefs and of their officers being steadily lowered in relation to the Civil Services. It therefore becomes important to examine some of these instances, understand the personalities on both sides and their impact on the future course of CMR.

EARLY DEFENCE MINISTERS

As mentioned, the nature of personalities at the helm impacts the extant Civil–Military balance. Sardar Baldev Singh, the first Defence Minister of India had a charming and genial personality. He let everyone 'get along with his job' to the extent that many thought that he was run by his Private Secretary, HC Sarin ICS, later to have a long and chequered career in the Defence Ministry.

As also stated earlier, the Defence Secretary during the initial post-Independence period was HM Patel, an ICS Officer of rare merit who enjoyed the full confidence of both the Prime Minister and Home Minister. (He was later the Finance Minister of India in the Janata Party led rule during 1977–80). The geniality of the then Defence Minister was from the bureaucrat's viewpoint a liability requiring them to put in place checks and balances to safeguard their Minister.

In the early days of Independent India, the Military, having been an instrument of power of the British was viewed with much suspicion. The Military's culture of secrecy did not help its cause. The first Chiefs of all three Services had all been British Officers who continued to practice their own military culture and traditions of service. The first Indian Officer to be appointed as C-in-C, Gen KM Cariappa, was also regarded as more of an Englishman in style and thought. *Sardar Patel had in fact opposed his appointment.* Unsure of the thought processes and thought behind the veil of secrecy, political leadership felt secure by enforcing a regimen of tight control of the Military, the reigns of which were held by a competent though compliant bureaucracy. *The Military, on its part, felt stifled.*

Furthermore, *the Military was first shorn of its rights to access the highest political authority, placed outside the apex decision-making apparatus followed by a sequence of control mechanisms which ensured that they could hardly move a sinew without the prior approval of the Ministry of Defence or through it, the Political Authority.*

The next two Defence Ministers were Gopalaswami Aiyyangar, an able administrator who true to expectations, was efficient and fair but was already at the time of assuming office very old and hence self-admittedly lacking in enthusiasm. He sadly died in harness and was succeeded by Dr Kailash Nath Katju, a leading political figure who was an affable personality, making friends easily and quickly endearing himself to all in the Ministry of Defence, but required to use a hearing aid. During his term too, the bureaucrats had to work hard to cover for his inability to take decisions. The Prime Minister assumed direct charge of the Defence Ministry for a while after Dr Katju's departure and thereafter appointed Mahavir Tyagi as the 'Minister of State for Defence Organisation', (a never-before-never-after terminology) under the general supervision of the Prime Minister.

Krishna Menon

Acclaimed as a remarkable scholar who made immense contribution to the formulation of India's Foreign Policy, Krishna Menon was Independent India's first High Commissioner to UK. A very close confidante and friend of the Prime Minister, he was made a Cabinet Minister without a Portfolio upon his return to India and in 1957 was appointed as Defence Minister. At that time, the Armed Forces had welcomed the move due to his reputation as a "doer" rather than a "watcher".

Menon's erudite eloquence and sharp intellect were, however, coupled with his untrusting nature. "The atmosphere in the Ministry was soon one of general suspicion with several officials at all levels indulging in carrying tales, often based on imagination and invention".

Another of Krishna Menon's negative traits was his acerbic tongue. His swipe such as referring to the Army as a "Parade Ground Army" while being the Defence Minister responsible to arm and equip it only lowered the morale of those who worked in proximity to him.

Henry Noel Brailsford, the British Left Wing Socialist who had supported the Indian freedom movement and was in communication with Mahatma Gandhi wrote about Krishna Menon:

> *I respect him for his hard work. But he is a sick man whose relations with his fellows can never be normal or happy. He seems always to create around himself an atmosphere of suspicion and intrigue. He split the Indian community in London and years it gave a painful exhibition of disunity".* Brailsford adds that *"He (Krishna Menon) is a man of first rate ability in certain directions, but his gift is not for dealing in a friendly and trustful way with others –whether equals or subordinates."*

Krishna Menon did not hide his contempt for the then prevalent culture of the Armed Forces, the accent and mannerisms of the military leadership or their social conduct.

I is also not that Menon's assessments were always inaccurate. Lt Gen Harbaksh Singh, erstwhile GOC-in-C Western Command, in his book *In the Line of Duty – A Soldier Remembers* quotes an instance where Menon while on a visit to Ferozepur to inaugurate a newly constructed accommodation for Officers and JCOs under a project titled 'Project Jyoti' had after unveiling the plaque turned to him and asked 'What's this? Do you call Shakespeare "Mr Shakespeare"?'[1] This was perhaps a rare occasion when a former Editor of Pelican Books at London that Menon was for once being exposed to Indian 'fauji' English language.

Relations between Krishna Menon and Gen KS Thimayya

All of Menon's formidable negative traits came to be applied in force in dealing with the then Chief of Army Staff Gen KS Thimayya. The twists and turns in their relationship was to have a severe bearing on the future relations between the Civil and the Military in India. Some of these are discussed below:

Assessing the China Threat

In 1959, the Chinese rejected the McMahon Line as the international boundary between China and India, and declared that Tibet was an "inalienable part" of China. They also extended their occupation of Aksai Chin to the heights overlooking Chushul and Rezang La. Gen Thimayya, conducted two War games: one each in the Western and Eastern theatres, which he personally supervised.

The War game in the Eastern theatre, named Ex Lal Qila and led by Major General S.P.P. Thorat concluded that the available troop and equipment levels were inadequate to contain or even delay the Chinese aggression. The other War game, Ex Sheel, conducted in Western Command, returned a similar assessment. 'The overall deduction of the study in early 1959 saw clearly the "*Chinese intention of crossing the Rubicon*" and that "*with the present state of development, the Chinese could launch a major incursion across any part of the border or create a situation where there would be the likelihood of a major operation taking place unless threatened by major retaliatory action by India.*"

Based on assessments of both exercises, Army Headquarters drew up a comprehensive proposal for increase in force levels, enhanced equipment and a revised deployment plan which was forwarded to the Ministry of Defence for approval.

These were days when the Defence Budget was limited (Rs 305 Crores for Financial year 1959–60), and wholly inadequate to meet the costs for the proposals projected. Krishna Menon, initially pended the proposal and it was after much persistence by Gen Thimayya that he finally agreed to consider and discuss them. A meeting was organised and the COAS was asked to explain the rationale for such a large force. Krishna Menon considered the demands made to be excessive and wanted them pruned down, which the COAS resisted.

In his book *Thimayya: An Amazing Life*, Brig CB Khanduri describes VK Krishna Menon having said to the Service Chiefs that he '*will not be bound by your sterile rules and procedures...and I know how to manage the services. I will call any one, any time and for that I need no permission from you*'.

Reason for Differences

The prime cause of differences, besides Menon's abrasive personality, was one of perspectives for, the Chiefs, principally Thimayya, advocated that the strategy to be adopted by India against the two perceived enemies it faced had to be dissuasive.[2]

Krishna Menon's perspective, however, was at variance to that of the Army Chief. He harped on India–China friendship and saw no need for the growth of the army at the rate that Thimayya regarded to be inescapable. Though he accepted the need for modernisation of the Army, this was however to be at a pace to be determined by him for inducting indigenous equipment and arms into Army service.

Thimayya meets the Prime Minister

In a chance social meeting with the Prime Minister not sought at his behest, Gen Thimayya "apologised for bothering him about defence matter when there was a full time minister and he was fully aware of the worsening situation on the border and of the imminence of hostilities" and drew his attention to *"the need to raise additional force for the northern borders, equip them and develop communications at priority". He also "pointed out how averse the defence minister was to those inescapable requirements, that had, indeed, been based on professional deliberations and analyses" besides highlighting "the lacunae in the defence set-up and how it needed to be urgently refurbished".*[3]

Appraising the Prime Minister of Krishna Menon's intransigence in accepting their considered views, he suggested the Prime Minister call the Defence Minister and emphasise the gravity of the situation besides reviewing the border situation. The Prime Minister, *on his part, insisted that Thimayya first talk to Krishna Menon stressing that bypassing a Minister may not be in order.* After Thimayya left, the Prime Minister called the Air and Naval Chiefs for a brief discussion with a view to ascertain their views. Upon his return, Krishna Menon had a meeting with the Prime Minister and when appraised of Gen Thimayya's meeting with the Prime Minister, fumed that he would ask the Chief to 'resign' and go, if he so wanted, adding – that he was not 'indispensable' and that the '*others' (the other two Chiefs) too could follow*. Nehru cautioned him to ensure that the Chiefs did not take a collective stand. *Menon then told Thimayya that he had no business to meet the Prime Minister without his specific approval to which Thimayya reiterated that it was the Prime Minister who desired to know about the preparedness, and the state of morale of the Services, which Menon did not accept and told Gen Thimayya that his discussion with the Prime Minister was 'downright disloyalty and impropriety'.* The conversation apparently ended with Menon telling Thimayya at the top of his voice that Thimayya had been disloyal to him and that there was '*no place for disloyal generals around*'.

The Prime Minister Intervenes

When Gen Thimayya's resignation letter reached before him, the Prime Minister called for him, assuaged and coaxed him by putting his arm around his shoulders, asking him why he hadn't met him rather than sending in his resignation. Nehru's famed charm worked and the meeting concluded with Thimayya being directed to withdraw the letter straightaway and to come back that evening with a letter of withdrawal. Soon, Thimayya met him again, Nehru admitted that Menon was indeed a "difficult man", but was doing service to defence which no one earlier had done to which Thimayya agreed, indicating that the problems were about his methods of "man-management".

When Chief's resignation episode was reported in the next morning's newspapers, Nehru, armed with the letter of withdrawal, assured Parliament that 'under our practice, the civil authority is, and must remain supreme' and referred to the army's 'fine mettle' and 'excellent morale' adding that the Chief should not have acted in the haste and manner he did. On his part, Thimayya said he had accepted the advice and the assurances of his Prime Minister and had withdrawn his resignation.

Consequences for Thimayya

The withdrawal of his resignation had its negative effects. Thimayya lost his moral hold over some of the officers who earlier deified him. *His resignation came to be viewed in terms of 'questioning civilian supremacy'.* Some felt that had he pushed ahead and resigned, the Government may well have been forced to do some serious thinking about the Chinese threat and made a "course correction".

There are some useful lessons to be learnt from the above episode. First, the survival instinct of the political class keeps their own interests uppermost. Second, it does not brook dissent, even on legitimate and valid grounds. Next, the episode concluded on the note of 'supremacy of the civil authority' being inviolate. **The Chiefs were now firmly under the control of the Defence Minister. They did not formally have direct access to the Prime Minister (and therefore the Union Cabinet) without going through the Defence Minister even on a matter of grave national importance.**

The 1962 Operations

Civil–Military Relations during the course of the 1962 Operations have been extensively written about by various Military experts and scholars. Neville Maxwell's revelations, even to the extent they are in the public domain are adequate to indicate a major disconnect between the political leadership and that of the military. The efforts and their futility on the part of Gen Thimayya to place his concerns before the Defence and Prime Ministers has been discussed. The successor COAS was obviously ineffective and was overawed and over shadowed by others who enjoyed proximity to the political leadership and who in turn were encouraged by the latter to bypass the system.

Adoption of the 'Forward Policy', 'Directions for eviction' that are included in the Terms of Reference of the Henderson Brooks report would both perhaps have not been issues if the leadership had a comprehensive and fair assessment of the situation on ground and the capabilities of our forces.

References to Henderson Brooks Report Available in Open Sources

Excerpts available in the public space include the following which have bearing on how effectively or otherwise the Civil and Military sides viewed the operations to be a national endeavour.

(a) 'The "Higher Direction of War" constituted by the Defence Ministry and the General Staff concerned itself with the odd reaction, here and there, and missed the main crux of the problem – The balance and strength of our Forces on the Defence line. Troops of a whole Brigade were disbursed to outposts that were militarily unsound and logistically unsupportable.'
Logistic air support for XXXIII Corps should as far as possible be from within XXXIII Corps allotment. Army Headquarters, however, had agreed to try and assist with additional support.'

Use of Air Power

An interesting and yet unanswered question relating to the 1962 debacle is as to why close air support was decided against. Marshal of the Air Force Arjan Singh (in one of his series of articles 'Down the Memory Lane' has written:

> *I am often asked why we did not take the offensive in 1962 operations when our Army was attacked by the Chinese. The Air Force took part in a big way in supply dropping and casualty evacuation operations. However it was decided by the Government that no offensive Air action would be undertaken. Had we done so with our fighter and bomber units in the crucial fighting even in two or three places, I think the outcome would have been somewhat different. In my opinion it was a mistake. We had adequate amount of Air Force and arrangements in the Assam valley, and we had the capability to use the Air Force effectively from the Air bases which were almost at sea level, a big advantage against those operating from bases at 14000 feet or so.*

Senior retired Air Force Officers stress the fact that the Chinese at that time had only two Air Force Bases, both located at very high altitude and could not operate any bombers from these bases. The Commanders at the time knew of the superiority they possessed. Some senior officers term the decision as 'chickening out' and attribute it to the fear that the Chinese would have retaliated by bombing Indian cities including Delhi.

> *The crucial issue still remains as to whether the Air Chief, who would have made a rational study on the Chinese capabilities for retaliation, the payloads their planes could have carried and how vulnerable their planes would have been if they indeed chose to target our cities, most particularly Delhi.*

The issue assumes significance when considered advice rendered by the Air Chief is disregarded.

Assistance from USA

An even more serious question is whether the plea Prime Minister Nehru made to the US President John Kennedy for twelve squadrons of F-104s and two squadrons of B-57 Bombers was made on the recommendation of the Air Chief. As several senior Air Force officers ask—Why these numbers? Who assessed these force requirements? Did the political authority think that up by their own or in consultation with other 'non-military' agencies?

Former Air Chief, ACM AY Tipnis was even more candid in his assessments. Addressing a Seminar on 'Five Decades of 1962 War' he alleged that 'Nehru had surrendered national security to realise his "ambition" to be a world leader'.[4] Emphasising that Nehru was 'the major contributor' to India's debacle, he added of having seen an Army Chief in those days being 'ticked off' like a school boy by Prime Minister Nehru for his petulance.

Post-War Fallout

Krishna Menon Resigns

Following the military debacle of 1962, there was an overwhelming sense of anger, shock and defeat that ran through the nation. The Defence Minister Krishna Menon was removed from the Cabinet, The Chief of Army Staff General PN Thapar sought retirement from service after taking full responsibility for the military failure, The Defence Secretary Pulla Reddi also retired from service and the Prime Minister took over charge of the Ministry of Defence and the Cabinet Secretary assumed charge as the Principal Defence Secretary. Gen JN Chaudhuri, who was GOC-in-C Southern Command was appointed as Chief of Army Staff at short notice.

Seen from the perspective of Civil-Military relations, Menon's resignation reflects acceptance of the onus of responsibility even for the military's actions though it came to be placed on the shoulders of the Defence Minister and not the Union Cabinet collectively.

In Support of Menon

Although there is almost complete unanimity amongst those in the Services fraternity towards Menon, his arrogance, attitude and the damage he caused to the Military, it is held by some on the Civil side that he was indeed a visionary who adhered to the principle that India should be Militarily strong. Towards this end, he had sought to develop India's defence Industrial base and convert Ordnance Factories into manufacturing hubs. His plans did not take off primarily due to his being denied adequate budgetary support by the then Finance Minister Morarji Desai. The root of evil is therefore Desai and his belief that as a land of 'ahimsa' India did not need an elaborate military. One former Intelligence Officer even mentioned of Desai considering spying to be evil and not providing support for such activities.

R Venkataraman, a former Defence Minister who went on to be the Finance Minister and eventually the President of India has acknowledged that '*Krishna Menon was the first to acknowledge that the defence industrial base, in the ultimate analysis, could not be divorced from the economic and industrial infrastructure of the country.*'

Rejuvenation Under Defence Minister Shri YB Chavan

Post Menon's removal from the Union Cabinet, Nehru convinced a reluctant Yashwantrao Balwantrao Chavan, the then Chief Minister of Maharashtra with the reputation of being an able administrator, to take charge of the Defence Ministry.

An assessment of the legacy Chavan inherited and the problems he faced at the time he joined the Defence Ministry is best obtained in the words of RD Pradhan, an IAS officer from the Maharashtra cadre who served as Chavan's Personal Secretary while he was Defence Minister (later to be Union Home Secretary). In Pradhan's words, '*Chavan was a shrewd politician and knew that from the moment he occupied the Defence Minister's chair, he would have to project himself as one in full control and quickly move to restore the proper relationship between the Army and the political leadership.*'[5]

To exemplify Chavan's skilful handling of officers and difficult situations, Pradhan gives the example of how Chavan handled the appointment of an ICS Officer PVR Rao, as the Defence Secretary without himself being consulted. The piquant situation was that Rao was hitherto Secretary to TT Krishnamachari who himself had hoped to be the Defence Minister. Upon joining the Defence Ministry, PVR Rao went up to the Defence Minister and mentioned that he knew his posting to the Ministry had been without the consent of the Minister and offered to proceed on long leave (to enable a suitable replacement being selected) but Chavan assured him by telling him '*You are my choice*' and winning him over.

In another incident, this time involving the then COAS Gen JN Chaudhuri who had sought to meet him urgently to complain about PVR Rao's blunt conduct with senior Army officers. Chavan asked Chaudhuri as to how many years he had served in the Army and whether after all those years it would be possible for him to change his style of working. Likewise, he stressed that PVR Rao too had many decades of service and even if he asked him to change his style, it would not be possible for him to do so. It would therefore be in everyone's interest to accept his style as an unchanging factor and move on.

There were two senior officers in the Ministry of Defence who carried a reputation of being 'Menon's boys'. In the tenure of the erstwhile Defence Minister, they enjoyed direct access to Menon and had his ear. There was pressure on Chavan to move them out but Chavan chose to call and let them know that they enjoyed his full confidence. Both continued to be retained in the Defence Ministry.

In Chavan's assessment, *one of the problem areas of Menon's regime was junior Army Officers being allowed direct access, even if informal, to the Defence Minister. Chavan was firm that the new Army Chief should be firmly in command of Army Headquarters and let all Principal Staff Officers know that while the Defence Minister was accessible to them, all proposals emanating from Army Headquarters must have the approval of the COAS. Although he patiently heard middle level officers, he encouraged them to follow established procedures in dealing with the Defence Ministry. He next sought to restore a proper and balanced relationship with Army Headquarters which had to begin at the highest level on both sides.*

In order to weld the three service chiefs and the Defence Secretary into a team, Chavan started the day with a Meeting attended by them and where when required the Cabinet Secretary and the Director Intelligence Bureau also attended. These "Morning Meetings were held not only to sort out problems but also to forge good working relationships".

Undoing the Menon Legacy

Another set of inflictions by Krishna Menon on the Services had been his seeking to demolish the careers of some otherwise excellent officers of the time who stood up to him. Two of these cases and how Chavan set their careers back on path are as follows:

Air Marshal PC Lal's case

Air Marshal PC Lal was one of the most outstanding officers of the Air Force who was clearly marked to be the Chief. He had, however, been deputed as managing Director of Indian Airlines during 1957–62. Krishna Menon had his own ideas about career management of senior officers whom he liked and did not want PC Lal to rejoin the Air Force He terminated his service on 30 September 1962. Chavan, who saw this case as one of great injustice called for Lal's case to be reviewed and with the Prime Minister's approval, reinstated him in the IAF. Chavan spoke to Morarji Desai, the Finance Minister, and got Lal's three month period of retirement regularised as leave without pay. This was a most unusual decision and remains perhaps the only case where an officer who actually retired was brought back into the service with full rank and all service entitlements.

Maj Gen Sam Manekshaw's Case

Another 'victim' of the former Defence Minister's antipathy and Lt Gen BM Kaul's intrigue' was (then) Maj Gen Sam Manekshaw, who, in Pradhan's words, was a 'a known anglophile'. He was alleged to have made some remarks in praise of the British and of being obliquely critical of the Congress Ministers at the Staff College at Wellington and faced an Inquiry into his indiscretions. Chavan called for the papers, quashed the proceedings and promoted Manekshaw to the rank of Lt Gen and appointed him as successor to Kaul as Commander of IV Corps, a decision which was universally welcomed.

Incident at HQ IV Corps: Chavan, Indira Gandhi and Sam Manekshaw

An incident not often quoted in Defence circles occurred at IV Corps during Lt Gen Manekshaw tenure as Corps Commander, which has a very significant bearing on CMR. On 05 December 1963 an operational briefing was scheduled at HQ 4 Corps for the Prime Minister who was then on visit to North East. The details of the incident are best left to be said in the words of RD Pradhan himself: '*it was winter and it was getting dark. Susheetal Banerjee, Deputy Secretary in the Cabinet Secretariat and I, followed the Prime Minister and Chavan. Mrs Indira Gandhi was a few steps behind. Lt Gen Manekshaw stopped at the entrance of the map room. Seeing Mrs Gandhi behind us, Susheetal and I gave her way at the entrance. Manekshaw stopped her and said "Madam, I am sorry you cannot enter the map room since you have not taken the Oath of Secrecy". Chavan immediately understood the situation. The Defence Minister did not want to let down his Corps Commander, so instead of talking directly to Mrs Gandhi, he looked at me and said "Ram, you better keep company of Mrs Gandhi".*

RD Pradhan goes on to add *"One could ... sense the seething anger building up within Indira Gandhi. She sat staring out of the window across her sofa. She "did not utter a word' during the over one and half hours she was in that room. "She felt greatly humiliated at being turned away at the entrance to the map room. She was right. Perhaps she would not have minded if the Corps Commander had told her discreetly earlier that she should not come for the Briefing".*[6]

Administrative Reform Commission 1967

It was in the Administrative Reforms Committee, set up by the Government in 1967 that for the very first time a formal consideration was done of two issues the Services have considered to be the root of all infirmities in the Defence Organisation—the need for an Integrated Ministry of Defence and of appointing a Chief of Defence Staff. The Commission had two Committees for Defence matters, headed each by two eminent personalities, Nawab Ali Yavar Jung and Shri SN Misra. Both these Committees considered that Integration of the Ministry of Defence and the Services Headquarters is required, but had different perceptions on the appointment of the CDS. The rationale for their respective views is evident in their notings as detailed in subsequent paragraphs.

On an Integrated Ministry of Defence

On the need for an Integrated Defence Ministry, Ali Yavar Jung states that '*the subordination of the Military to the civil power should be interpreted in the political and not in the bureaucratic sense*' SN Misra endorses this view point in his own recommendation that '*the principle of civilian control over the Defence machinery should be interpreted to mean not bureaucratic of civil service control but essentially ultimate political control by the Parliament and the Cabinet*'.[7]

Ali Yavar Jung's comment on duplication that '*there is the factor to consider seriously of duplication of work which constitute a waste, both financial and in terms of talent and time. Such duplication occurs mostly in the name of coordination and supervision, it contributes little except delay*' rings true even till this day.

On the Appointment of a CDS

On the appointment of the CDS, though they were not on the same page, Ali Yavar Jung felt that the Services '*should retain their separate identities but all operational matters need to be coordinated and operations eventually integrated. This alone would ensure a single line of ultimate professional responsibility; without it the Services would not be able, all of a sudden, to bring about the effective unified command which is required in war. We believe there is a need for a Chief of Defence Staff who would be the coordinator and the executive at the top echelon of all the three operational commands. The structure in peacetime should conform to the requirements of war.*'

Smt Sharda Mukherji, the widow of late Air Marshal Subroto Mukherji, was a member of the Committee and strongly dissented on the issue of appointing a CDS. This was also the view of the Chairman, Shri SN Misra, and the opinion expressed before the Committee by the then Air and Naval Chiefs. The deliberations of the Committee throw light as to how far back the steady opposition, particularly in the IAF, to the institution of the CDS goes. (A little known fact about Smt. Sharda Mukherjee is that apart from being the widow of the former Air Chief, she was born Sharda Pandit and a niece of Ranjit Pandit, the husband of Vijayalakshmi, Prime Minister Nehru's sister).

Field Marshal Sam Manekshaw

General (later Field Marshal) Sam Manekshaw's tenure as Chief of the Army Staff coincided with that of Smt Indira Gandhi as Prime Minister. Both were very strong personalities with a degree of mutual understanding and regard for each other. Yet, according to one former Bureaucrat, it is highly unlikely that she would have let bygones be bygones on the earlier rebuff by Manekshaw at Tezpur, when he did not allow her to enter the Operations Room at the Corps Headquarters.

Lt Gen Depinder Singh (Retd), erstwhile GOC-in-C Southern Command who had earlier been Military Assistant to the Field Marshal has recounted some of these in his Biography of the Field Marshal titled *Field Marshal Sam Manekshaw: Soldiering with Dignity*, which are discussed hereunder:

Opportunity for a CDS missed

Giving details of one such instance, Gen Depinder Singh writes,

> *On a date prior to 26th January 1972 the Prime Minister had ordered that the Army Chief be promoted to the rank of Field Marshal and appointed Chief of Defence Staff, and that the appointment be made on the morning of Republic Day 1972. For some unfathomable reason, that was not done thereupon the Prime Minister directed that the announcement be made on the 28th January 1972 as the Chief (the Field Marshal) and the other two Chiefs were being awarded the Padma Vibhushan that afternoon. This too fell through and nothing more was heard by us. Over the years, the bureaucracy has evolved a perfect system to stall, what, to them, is an unwholesome direction. A very simple expedient is resorted to: a point concerning one service will be referred to the other two services and their views sought. If one or more services send a negative reply, the project is consigned to the dustbin as being 'unacceptable to the other two services'. I have no doubt that this proposal too met this fate as though the navy was agreeable to Sam's promotion; the Air Force was vehemently against it, citing, as a very unconvincing reason, that this would amount to belittling the Air Force's achievements.*[8]

Who is the Government?

Detailing his own 'tiff' with an official of the Ministry of Defence on an issue at the root of Civilian control over the Military, Lt Gen Depinder Singh mentions that on the 2nd or 3rd January a note was handed over to him, which *'sought the Chief's approval to the announcement it was intending to make that evening over the radio and to the press, announcing the name of the New Chief. I showed this note to the Chief who asked me to take it back to the JS(G) who had initiated it, with a request that the announcement be made the following evening as the Chief himself wished to ring up General Bewoor the next morning to break the news and congratulate him. I walked across and saw the official concerned and conveyed the request to him. Why, he wanted to know, was it necessary for the Chief to telephone General Bewoor when this should really be done by the Government'.*

What followed is really interesting. In Gen Depinder Singh's words, '*When I asked whether the Field Marshal was not equally a part of the same*

Government, I got the reply that Government meant the Defence Secretary. On my pointing out that if the Chief was a soldier so the Secretary was a bureaucrat and the Government really meant the elected representatives of the people who in this case should be the Defence Minister. I was given a baleful glare and the cryptic answer that we should not quibble over such matters'. It is the conclusion of the episode that mattered, adds Lt Gen Depinder Singh, adding *that 'the announcement was made the next day after the Chief spoke to (Gen) Bewoor'.* It is perhaps the charisma and personality of the Field Marshal that prevailed over bureaucratic dogma and blinkered adherence to precedence and sham protocol. Also ominous is the underlying message that the 'Services' including the 'Chief' are not integral to the body politic of the Government.

Field Marshal's Fall from Favour

Even more significant are the details Lt Gen Depinder Singh provides which relate to how the Field Marshal fell out of grace of the political leadership who he worked so closely with. The first instance he mentions relates to an interview the Field Marshal gave to a Delhi weekly in which two responses by him led to controversy.

One: London is my favourite city and I feel at home there.

Two: "Jinnah had asked me to join the Pakistan Army in 1947. If I had, you would have had a defeated India".

In the course of the outrage in parliament on these remarks, particularly the latter, there were also references made to excerpts in a book *Fighting General* by Tom Pocock, which mentioned that in a meeting with Gen Sir James Walker of the British Army with Gen Manekshaw in the course of an informal meeting while the Field Marshal was passing through India, they shared perceptions about politicians and the quantum of interference they should be allowed in Defence matters. Lt Gen Depinder Singh adds here that while the Field Marshal could never be accused of doubting the supremacy of the elected representatives, he could not tolerate interference in routine matters as discipline would certainly have suffered had he allowed it. An Army without discipline is merely a rabble.

NOTES

1. Lt Gen Singh, Harbaksh, *In the Line of Duty – A Soldier Remembers* (New Delhi: Lancer Publications, 2000), p. 306.
2. Khanduri, C.B., *Thimayya, An Amazing Life*, New Delhi: Centre for Armed Historical Research United Service Institution of India and Knowledge World, pp. 395–9.
3. Ibid.
4. 'Ex-IAF chief Tipnis blames Nehru for defeat in 1962 China War', *The Times of India*, 20 Nov 2012.
5. Pradhan, R.D., 'Debacle to Resurgence Y B Chavan: Defence Minister (1962-66)', Asiatic, 2013.
6. Pradhan, R.D., 'Debacle to Revival: Y B Chavan as Defence Minister, 1962-65' (New Delhi: Orient Longman, 1999).
7. 'Historical Overview', *Review of the Management of Defence*, Ministry of Defence 2000, p. 35.
8. Lt Gen Singh, Depinder, *Field Marshal Sam Manekshaw: Soldiering with Dignity*, (Dehradun: Natraj Publishers, 2003 (reprinted 2005)), p. 204.

CHAPTER 5

BOGEY OF A COUP

An issue not generally discussed in open forums is of the possibility of a 'Coup' by the Military in India. Even discussing the subject is taboo within the Military. It is former Chief of the Army Staff, General S. Padmanabhan who has not only raised this issue upfront but also elaborated upon it. He postulates the necessary circumstances in this context. His book *A General Speaks* first defines the phenomenon of the military usurping the authority to govern the country to be 'Praetorianism' a word derived from the 'Praetorian Guards' a body of troops who, in ancient Rome were charged with the responsibility of protecting the Emperor but instead, specialised in making and unmaking emperors. Today Praetorianism is defined as a situation where 'the military class of a society exercises independent power by virtue of an actual or threatened use of force'.

This kind of military intervention, General Padmanabhan elaborates, '*is the consequence of the interplay of two sets of factors in a given domestic and external environment. For a military coup to fructify, both these factors must be mixed optimally forming a critical mass as it might be said in nuclear science, they being:*

- *(a) The military and its capacity as well as its propensity to intervene.*
- *(b) The state of the society including the socio-political economic situation and their net effect on the polity*'.[1]

The underlying precondition is that a Coup cannot be organised at the will of the Military alone. The social political and economic state of a nation has to be in a state of such disarray or turmoil for the general population to accept the intervention as a welcome redeemer. The recent incidents in Turkey underscore this aspect.

Civilian control of the military, General Padmanabhan goes on to emphasise, '*is a bulwark against its intervention if the control has been institutionalised in an enlightened and not arbitrary manner. If the control is perceived as arbitrary, even highly professional officer corps like in the German French or Pakistani armies could turn Praetorian thus defeating the very aim of civilian control".*[2]

Both the two pre-requisite factors mentioned by General Padmanabhan, i.e. the capacity of the Armed Forces and the politico-socio-economic despondence that society is bearing never existed.

INSTANCES FROM THE PAST

In this backdrop, it becomes relevant to examine some recorded instances where the Political leadership was either spooked or was led to believe that there was sinister scheming on the part of some senior Army Officers.

January 1961

The first of these instances goes back to January 1961. This was the time when Krishna Menon was the Defence Minister and his relations with the three Chiefs had reached a never before low. There were rumours of the then COAS, Gen Thimayya, planning a takeover for which 30 January, death anniversary of Mahatma Gandhi, had been fixed. The rumour arose due to Gen Thimayya having ordered the move of a Division from Ambala to Delhi. This move apparently synchronised with the move to Delhi of an Armoured Brigade then located at Mathura. The orders for movement of the Brigade had been issued directly to the Division Commander with even Principal Staff Officers at Army Headquarters being oblivious of both, the move itself and the reasons for which it had been ordered. The move orders were soon countermanded and the Division returned to its home station Ambala.

There is an ominous parallel that these moves have with the more recent instance of troop movements on 'exercise' from Hissar and Mathura towards Delhi on the night of the 16th January 2012, pertinently, was the day General VK Singh, the then Chief of the Army Staff, had petitioned the Supreme Court of India on the well-known issue of his date of birth. In the latter instance too, troops were asked to return to their stations and revised instructions regarding Government authorisation prior to authorising such movements have since been issued.

The significant lesson to be learnt from both instances is that notwithstanding their loud pronouncements in praise of the 'apolitical' nature of our Armed Forces and of their contributions to maintain peace and tranquillity on the borders, the fact remains that deep down, the political class remains apprehensive and very jittery about the military's possible intentions and a lurking mistrust of the Military still exists in some deep mental crevices of the political class.

March 1961

A few weeks prior to his retirement on 07 May 1961, General Thimayya visited the Kumaon Regimental Centre at Ranikhet. At the farewell function held in his honour, Gen SPP Thorat allegedly made statements critical of the Government and urged the troops to be loyal to their Chief without, as is customary, exhorting them to be loyal to the Government and the Constitution of India. The plea he made to the soldiers was to the effect that, 'Do not let Thimayya go away', thereby an appeal to them to be loyal to their Chief with no word on their loyalty to the Government or the Constitution of India is what seemed to have pressed a panic button in the corridors of Civilian power. Soon afterwards, Gen Thorat himself left the Army.

This incident resulted in the already soured and tenacious relations between Gen Thimayya and the Government, becoming even more acerbic. It also cast a doubt on the character and reputation of another very fine officer, Gen SPP Thorat who may well have been a victim of some imaginative reporting by a fertile mind.

June 1964

Lt Gen Harbaksh Singh VrC, erstwhile GOC-in-C Western Command, in his book *In the Line of Duty – A Soldier Remembers* recounts another interesting instance when this fear of the coup comes to the fore. He says:

> *In June 1964 there was a rumour among officers of the Corps that I was due to be posted as Army Commander Eastern Command, to Calcutta. This soon changed to Western Command at Simla. The reason for this change, I was told later, was that the Defence Ministry suspected that the Chief of Army Staff General Chaudhuri and the Army Commander Western Command Lt Gen Manekshaw, his buddy, were conniving together to perform a coup against the Government.*[3]

To be fair to the Field Marshal it is necessary to also quote the following extracts from Maj General Shubhi Sood's book *Leadership Field Marshal Sam Manekshaw:*

> *The circumstances under which he (then Lt Gen Sam Manekshaw) was posted to Eastern Command as narrated by Sam were somewhat different. He (Sam) told me that Gen Chaudhuri the then Chief of the Army Staff went to lecture at the Staff College at Wellington, in May 1964 when Pandit Nehru was critically ill. Before leaving for Wellington he wrote a letter to Sam Manekshaw...and left it in a sealed envelope with Gen Wadalia the Vice Chief of Army Staff with instructions that should something happen to Pandit Nehru, the letter was to be delivered to Manekshaw. On 27th May 1964 Pandit Nehru died. Gen Wadalia rang up Manekshaw and said to him...the Chief has left a sealed letter with me and I am supposed to read out his instructions to you. Please come on the scrambler and I will read them out to you.... The Chief in his wisdom had felt that should Pandit Nehru pass away, it might lead to a situation of strife in the capital and this would entail employment of the Army to bring the situation under control. Since there were no troops located or available at Delhi, he had directed Manekshaw, the Western Army Commander to move to Delhi with his advance Headquarters along with 4 Infantry Division from Ambala and the 50 parachute Brigade from Agra. When this was conveyed to Manekshaw, he objected vehemently and said that this was not the right thing to do and would send wrong signals to the polity and the country. The Vice Chief told Sam '...my job is to convey the instructions of the Chief and you will have to speak to*

> *him if you have anything to say...'. Sam thus put his down his objections in writing and sent them to the Chief while carrying out the orders of the Chief.*
>
> *Once the new Prime Minister assumed office and things settled down, the Government asked the Chief as to why troops were moved in this manner to Delhi. Gen JN Chaudhuri instead of narrating what had transpired, told them that Sam did this on his own initiative.*[4]

It was from the then Defence Minister, YB Chavan that Sam got to know of this and he accosted the Chief as to why he had to say this, adding, 'I had all along objected to your idea and was against doing anything like this. I even wrote to you'. Gen Chaudhuri replied, 'Sam, I had to say something and this was the first thing that came to my mind'. As a consequence of this Gen Manekshaw was moved to Calcutta as GOC-in-C Eastern Command...[5]

Another interesting episode, which again brings out the effectiveness of these 'Agencies', that Maj Gen Shubhi Sood has mentioned:

> *Sam was very fond of dancing and believed that this acts as an antidote to stress. Sometime before the (1971) War, while there was intense activity at the Army Headquarters and the Ministry of Defence, the Chief was seen dancing at 'Chinois', a Chinese specialty Restaurant at the Oberoi Hotel in Delhi. This sighting of the Chief was duly reported by some Agency to the Prime Minister. The next morning it so happened that he had a meeting with the Prime Minister in her office. Once discussions on the official business were over, Mrs Gandhi brought up the subject and gently advised him to avoid dancing with pretty girls late into the night at public places. All this while the Chief remained calm and listened to the lecture of the prime Minister.. Once she had finished he asked her if she knew who the lady was. On being told no he said "Prime Minister, the lady with whom I was seen dancing is my daughter!!" Both of them (thereafter) had a hearty laugh.*

Interestingly, what emerges from these instances is the omnipresence of the 'Agencies' and their access to the 'ear' of the political class. The reporting to the Prime Minister of such personal activities of a Chief, and certainly regarding other very senior officers, reveals the close watch they are subject to by Security and Intelligence agencies, as is bound to be. It is the potential for damage that inaccurate or incomplete reporting holds is where the problem arises. In this case, the Field Marshal had an early occasion to clear the air with the Prime Minister. Others may not be so fortunate and face a 'black mark' even if they had no negative traits and their actions or even choice of words were entirely well-intentioned.

There is an interesting revelation in Gen Depinder Singh's book, which throws light on the Politico–Military relations of the time. This relates to the Defence Minister Babu Jagjivan Ram who enjoyed enormous popularity, often hinted to the Chief to 'join' him. The Chief 'understood his motive which was to align with him against the Prime Minister, but the Chief chose to deflect his answer by appearing to misinterpret the suggestion and replying that as Chief he was 'already joined to his Minister'. The episode, however, reveals that even at the highest level of the Political elite, the support of the Military is regarded as a great source of strength.

Further, another 'inside revelation' comes from Lt Gen PN Hoon in his book *Unmasking Secrets of Turbulence Midnight Freedom to a Nuclear Dawn*, in which he writes:

> *Many Facets of Giani Zail Singh and General Sundarji have been discussed regarding their plan to dismiss Rajiv Gandhi in May-June 1987 which they could not succeed. When a question was asked why Giani Zail Singh chose not to finally dismiss Rajiv Gandhi, but he replied, The first reason was that he had asked Rajiv to apologise to him which he did and the second reason was that if he had dismissed Rajiv and appointed a successor, the successor may have been a weak person which could have led to a transfer of power from a democratically elected Government to the Armed Forces. What did he mean??? The plan was hatched by late Sh. Vidya Charan Shukla and Sundarji. Vidya Charan Shukla, then the Minister of Information and Broadcasting who came and met me in my office in Chandigarh when I was the Commander-in-Chief of the Western Army. He told me that if Rajiv Gandhi was to be removed what Role would the Indian Army Play? I told him that it is shocking that you had the guts to come to me. Never come again. I was quite clear that this cannot be allowed to happen. I immediately flew to Delhi shared this information with Rajiv Gandhi as to what was going on in the presence of Late Shri Gopi Arora and simultaneously directed my Chief of Staff Lt General Garewal that NO troops as ordered by Army Head Quarters will move or enter Delhi. A signal had been received by my Headquarters from Army Head Quarters to move three Para Commando Battalions to Delhi under Delhi Area Commander.*[6]

IS A COUP FEASIBLE?

Theoretically, the combined strength of all the Armed Forces personnel is not in itself adequate to enforce any control across the country. Assuming that all of the Defence Services themselves are fully on board, there would be support of other Forces—the Paramilitary and the State Forces, which, many in the military consider having been set up to be countervailing forces to preclude such a prospect. This too, is a far cry. Unlike elsewhere in the neighbourhood, the apolitical culture of the Indian Military has a very strong streak, as is their pride and self-righteousness. This will never allow them to comply with an illegal order.

It is a view in the Military that the threat of a coup is a bogey raised by some who mattered in the Police Forces, who regularly played upon the fears of the political class to build up a fear phobia against the Armed Forces. This gave them the patent to watch the military closely and report every event of any significance to the political leadership. The flip side to this was that an entire 'countervailing combine' of Central and Police Forces, almost equal in numbers to the 'teeth' of the Armed Forces had been built up over the years, all under the control of the Ministry of Home Affairs. Without collusion between these Forces and the Military there is no way that the 'critical mass' that Gen Padmanabhan considered necessary for any intervention would ever form.

INDIA IS NOT PAKISTAN

To understand as to why a coup in India is not possible, a comparison with Pakistan is relevant. The politicisation of the military in that country took place due to it having upon itself to confront a larger state with inadequate resources on an assurance from its military of victory. A failed coup in 1951 made the Prime Minister, Liaqat Ali Khan, to co-opt General Ayub Khan into the Cabinet which opened the Army and the Armed Forces to involvement in the affairs of the state generally handled by the civil government. Such prospects have been non-existent in India, then and now.

THE MILITARY'S APPREHENSIONS

The threat of coup is hence a mere bogey, mainly raised without qualms by various 'Agencies' or civil servants to sustain deep apprehensions about the military in the minds of the political class, a fear that seemed to come to fore in reaction to the 16th January 2012 troop movements.

A 'gainer' in the perpetuation of this fear of the coup has largely been the police forces. The several Central police organisations raised over the years have placed under the control of the Ministry of Home Affairs adequate force strength to pose a challenge at least numerically, to a mutinous military.

NOTES

1. General Padmanabhan, S. (Retd.), *A General Speaks* (New Delhi: Manas Publications, 2005), p. 103.
2. Ibid., p. 107.
3. Lt. Gen Singh, Harbaksh, *In the Line of Duty – A Soldier Remembers* (New Delhi: Lancer Publications, 2000), p. 323.
4. Maj Gen Sood, Shubhi, *Leadership Field Marshal Sam Manekshaw* (Noida: SDS Publishers, 2006), p. 42.
5. Ibid., p. 43.
6. Lt Gen Hoon, P.N., *Unmasking Secrets of Turbulence Midnight Freedom to a Nuclear Dawn* (New Delhi: Manas Publications).

CHAPTER 6

MANAGING THE MILITARY LEADERSHIP

THE SELECTION OF SERVICE CHIEFS AND SENIOR COMMANDERS

There are three cardinal factors on which selections to all apex appointments in the Government are made: 'seniority', 'merit' and 'other matters'. Though 'seniority' and 'merit' underlay selections for promotion to higher ranks to the senior most rungs of the Armed Forces, when it comes to Apex appointments, the selection process expands beyond these criteria, to include any or all of such additional inputs on personal or professional aspects that the democratically elected authority would deem appropriate and necessary to take into account. This is a cardinal dimension of Civilian political control over the military.

It is in this backdrop that some 'contentious' selection decisions and how some notable emergent issues concerning Service Chiefs had been managed need to be examined. Some of these decisions are still recounted in Military circles as ones where outstanding officers had been 'done in'.

SUPERSESSIONS

Air Marshal Shiv Dev Singh (1972)

Considered as the most operationally experienced Commander of his time, Air Marshal Shiv Dev Singh was not only in-charge of the IAF during the liberation of Goa, he was the Vice Chief of Air Staff during the 1971 Ops and is credited with master-minding the entire air operations during these operations. Many in the Air Force still believe that though the then CAS, Air Chief Marshal PC Lal is given the credit for the Air Force success, it actually goes in large measure to Air Marshal Shiv Dev Singh.

The narrative goes that as the Senior most Air Force Officer, Air Marshal Shivdev Singh's appointment as successor to Air Chief Marshal Lal was regarded as a foregone one. The then Defence Minister, Jagjivan Ram, was even supposed to have called on telephone and congratulated him after his appointment had been approved.

For some unknown reasons, there was an overnight change and Air Marshal OP Mehra was appointed on promotion as the successor to Air Chief Marshal Lal. Air Marshal Shiv Dev Singh gracefully retired from service without rancour and never spoke about his supersession. There is no one with know of the period existing who has vivid memories of events of the time. Some senior Air Force officers, rather unsurely mention that at the root of the supersession were Defence Deals. There were also whispers of "Jaguar", but no details. Hence the supersession needs to be accepted as having been taken in the best national interests.

Supersession of Lt Gen PS Bhagat (1972)

In 1972, Lt Gen PS Bhagat, a winner of the Victoria Cross for gallantry and a very popular and professionally outstanding officer was side-stepped as the Chairman of the Damodar Valley Corporation. The incumbent Chief, Gen Sam Manekshaw, was granted an extension in service, as was Lt Gen GG Bewoor, his successor.

A reference to this supersession, made in disregard to the recommendation of the then Chief has been detailed in Lt Gen Depinder Singh's book in which he writes:

> *In the first week of January 1973, the Government decided that Lt Gen GG Bewoor., PVSM the Southern Army Commander would be the next Chief in succession to the Field Marshal who would relinquish office on 15 January 1973. I might add here that the Chief's choice, which he*

> *could only convey to the Prime Minister verbally was of Lt Gen PS Bhagat VC. Mrs Gandhi was, however, under tremendous pressure from Mr YB Chavan to grant General Bewoor an extension beyond his retirement date and appoint him as COAS. During one discussion on the subject between the Chief and the Prime Minister, she mentioned that one reason why Bewoor was preferred over Bhagat was that the latter was pro-Sikh. On the Chief's asking how that conclusion was reached she remarked that there were numerous photographs of Bhagat with Sikh troops. The Chief's explanation that Bhagat, being a Colonel of the Sikh Light Infantry naturally appeared in these photographs, evidently was not accepted.*[1]

There is no denying that this supersession caused a deep impact on the psyche of Sikh officers who came to believe for a very long time that the 'top job' was not for one of them, whatever be their achievements'. This grievance of the Sikh community was only partially assuaged many years later when Gen JJ Singh took over as Chief of the Army Staff in 2005.

Perceptions on why Gen Bhagat was side-stepped in a deft move to ensure a different set of successors abound. Besides the 'Maharashtra' connection that Lt Gen Depinder Singh mentions of, there is also a 'Kashmir' connect some mention as the natural successor to Gen GG Bewoor was to be Lt Gen TN Raina. The other and somewhat plausible theory relates to Gen Bhagat being the (junior) co-author of the Henderson Brooks Report. The 'harsh' line the Report had supposedly taken on the role of the then political leadership did not exactly endear him to their next of kin. Some also mention the extravagant lifestyle of the Bhagats had caught the attention of the 'Agencies' whose Reports would have only added to the other negatives that led to Gen Bhagat being passed over. Nevertheless, it needs to be mentioned that Gen Bhagat was appointed Chairman of the Damodar Valley Corporation where he worked with zeal to increase power production until his untimely death just ten months into that appointment.

Supersession of Lt Gen SK Sinha (1983)

The supersession in 1983 of the then VCOAS and senior most Army claimant to the appointment of the COAS, Lt Gen SK Sinha in favour of Lt Gen AS Vaidya is one that is still quoted, mainly for having been driven by considerations of 'tractability' over 'merit'. It assumes other hues such as Armoured Corps over Infantry, 'Command experience over excellence in Staff, etc. For a dispassionate and fact-based understanding, it is best to draw from the authorship of two of the principal protagonists in the script and draw one's own perceptions on why it merits or otherwise.

Gen KV Krishna Rao, the then COAS who Gen Sinha was the senior most to succeed and later to be Governor of Nagaland and Jammu & Kashmir states has, in his book *In the Service of the Nation* written:

> *Towards the end of my tenure a controversy would arise over the appointment of my successor. The Government announced that Lt Gen AS Vaidya, GOC-in-C Eastern Command, was appointed as the new Chief of the Army Staff. This meant that Lt Gen SK Sinha, the Vice Chief of the Army staff was superseded. Unfortunately, a controversy was created on this issue. Allegations were made that the supersession was motivated by political considerations that Lt Gen Vaidya was a sickly person and medically unfit that seniority had been overlooked despite Lt Gen Sinha being fit in all respects, that there was division in the officer ranks of the Army on this account, and so on. In view of the likely adverse impact of such propaganda on the Army and in order to facilitate a smooth changeover, Lt Gen Vaidya starting on the right foot, I tried to correct some of the misconceptions".*[2]
>
> *In the normal course I would not have written about this, but I feel a clarification is necessary in the interest of truth and justice. Sometime before I was due to retire, the Prime Minister had called me up and asked me as to who should take over from me. As it was not usual for an incumbent Chief to be consulted I expressed surprise and sought some time to analyse the confidential dossiers of all the officers eligible, to which the Prime Minister agreed.*
>
> *I then sent for these dossiers, made thorough analysis of the career profile of the officers concerned from the time they were selected as cadets to the time they held the Army Commander/Vice Chief appointments. This included the grades obtained in Annual Confidential reports, the strong and weak points reflected therein, the results of various training courses, the performance in wars, the performance in counter-insurgency operations, the honours and awards received and other details. The factual analysis gave a comprehensive idea of the career profile of each officer".*

> *"I then gave this, along with the dossiers to the Prime Minister, who studied the analysis in my presence and remarked that it was clear that Lt Gen Vaidya should be the next Chief according to the professional performance of the officers concerned. She would no doubt have consulted the Defence Minister also. At the appropriate time, orders were issued appointing Lt Gen Vaidya as the new Chief. Without going into the confidential aspects of the career profile of the officers concerned – which are absolutely clear, I should mention that as far as I know, there were no political considerations and the selection was purely based on merit, that Lt Gen Vaidya was absolutely fit being in medical category AYE-1, and that there was no question of dissentions in the Army as the selection was made purely on a professional basis. In any case, the record is available with the government. I should mention that I had nothing personal against Sinha, that I ensured justice was done in his earlier promotions and that he is as good a fried as anyone else.*
>
> *Such controversies were raised in the past also, on certain occasions when a new Chief was selected. Unfortunately, this happens due to disinformation by vested interests, not only in the Army but also in the civil services and polity. It needs to be realised that when a person reaches an Army Commander or equivalent level, his attainments would be quite significant. However, there are six officers of that level and only one vacancy of the Chief. The government has to be extremely careful in selecting a person for this vital appointment. It will be agreed that no consideration other than comparative merit should form the basis for this selection. As far as I am aware, the selections in the past were generally made on this consideration, and thus, when exposed to a war, those concerned by and large vindicated the confidence reposed in them. These included Thimayya, Chaudhuri and Manekshaw. There was of course, an odd exception".*[3]

This version of Gen Krishna Rao needs to be juxtaposed against what Gen SK Sinha has himself written in his autobiography *A Soldier Recalls* under a Chapter titled 'Supersession".

Commencing from how he got the news of his supersession, Gen Sinha states that he was *"in Gen Krishna Rao's room discussing some cases...when a telephone call came to him and I heard only what he spoke. I did not know who was talking at the other end. (Gen Rao) enquired if he could now make the announcement. Apparently he got a reply in the affirmative. He put the telephone down and asked the Military Assistant on the intercom to get him Eastern Army Commander (Vaidya) on the line. Thereafter he turned to me and in a very matter of fact manner and said that the Government had decided that Arun Vaidya should succeed him. I was not taken aback so much by the fact that contrary to all previous indications and beliefs, I was to be superseded, but by the attitude of Krishna".*[4]

In Civil–Military terms, both on principles and procedure, there are several pertinent issues that arise 'or be perceived from' this controversy.

First, though Gen Rao does not mention specifically and Gen Sinha clearly believes, the Government did call for a revised recommendation from the COAS. **The recommendation of the outgoing Chief was hence not overruled but he was called upon to alter, under what Gen Sinha believes, to be political pressure, to recommend a candidate who suited the Government's requirements. Second, the reputation of having a forceful personality and high intellectual ability are not necessarily positive attributes. Thirdly, there is zero tolerance for even a whiff of political connections especially with parties or personages inimical in the Government and its leadership.**

Though this supersession had taken place way back in 1983, in conclusion, it needs to be mentioned that the overwhelming impression in the Armed Forces, as reflected in the very prompt responses of interviewees of the Study is that Generals KV Krishna Rao and AS Vaidya had somewhere compromised in favour of the then ruling dispensation. Many have mentioned of the fruits reaped by the former by being appointed to gubernatorial appointments for more than one term post his retirement from Army Service.

Supersession of Air Marshal MM Singh (1988)

The Air Force has its own equivalent case of ACM SK Mehra who too reached the highest slot in the IAF by superseding a most well-regarded and highly acclaimed professional, Air Marshal MM Singh in 1988. While Air Marshal MM Singh had a formidable reputation as a high class professional and an ace pilot.

The professional superiority of Air Marshal MM Singh came to be established when the IAF conducted Op Hammerblow, a major exercise in March 1988 in which the Western Air Command (WAC), then headed by the senior most AOC-in-C, Air Marshal MM Singh and the South Western Air Command (SWAC) commanded by Air Marshal S.K. (Polly) Mehra took part. The WAC triumphed in the Exercise reinforcing the candidature of Air Marshal MM Singh to succeed Air Chief Marshal Dennis La Fontaine. However, against all expectations, Air Marshal Mehra's name was announced as the successor on 20 Jun 1988.

Air Marshal MM Singh, who was on tour to J&K at the time the announcement was made returned and submitted his papers for premature retirement from service with effect from 31 July 1988, the day the incumbent Air Chief was due to retire. The supersession of a professionally competent and popular officer had, '*sent ripples of disappointment through the corridors of Vayu Bhawan*'. It was due to 'other issues' relating to personal propriety, reportedly of his 'companion' not being married to him that compelled the Government to overlook his otherwise rightful claim to be the Air Chief.

Unlike the supersession of Lt Gen SK Sinha where operational experience was forwarded as a justification, Air Marshal MM Singh's operational record compared favourably with that of Air Marshal Mehra. His command of Western Air Command (WAC), which had operational command over 25 of the IAF's 39 combat squadrons and an operational area as large as that of the Pakistan Air Force, was considered very successful. The reasons for the supersession hence lay elsewhere.

The build up to this supersession makes an interesting study and reveals that the decision, far from being a sudden development was a much planned one.

At first, the Defence Ministry had asked the Air Chief, ACM Marshal Dennis La Fontaine, for a pen picture of the two contenders. La Fontaine had reportedly assessed that while Air Marshal MM Singh had an outstanding career from the operational point of view, Air Marshal SK Mehra, having served more years in Air Headquarters, knew the administrative ropes well. Once the Government had made up its mind on its choice for the next Air Chief attempted to persuade Air Marshal Singh to resign on his own volition, which he refused. This was done both through ACM Marshal La Fontaine, who informed him that the then Defence Minister KC Pant had told him of Government's intention to appoint Air Marshal Mehra as the next Air Chief. However, Air Marshal Singh refused. Thereafter, the Defence Secretary, Shri SK Bhatnagar, who was himself due to retire from service on 31 May 1988 called Air Marshal Singh over and asked him to resign before Air Marshal Mehra took over so as to save both the Government and himself any embarrassment. Air Marshal Singh again did not oblige but informed his colleagues of the pressure being put on him to quit the service.

The Defence Ministry declined to comment either on the pressure put on Air Marshal Singh or on his meeting with the Defence Secretary. The then Defence Secretary denied that he ever asked Air Marshal Singh to put in his papers. But along with the appointment of Air Marshal Mehra as the next Chief, there were suggestive news items regarding Air Marshal Singh's personal life, particularly a 'romantic involvement' that the Government considered with seriousness. While Air Force officers were aghast at the deliberate slurring of a senior officer who commanded much respect and there were questions as to why in that case, was he allowed to remain as AOC-in-C of the WAC for almost three years, these were never answered.

A very practical aspect of the exercise of Civilian Control over the Military is that for selection to apex ranks, even the slightest misconduct in personal life could become the basis to deny a selection.

There are, however, instances of government having invited criticism upon itself for ignoring certain officers who clearly stood out professionally. In 1961, for instance, had Lt Gen SPP Thorat been appointed his senior in place of Gen PN Thapar it may have filled the acute leadership deficit during the 1962 Operations.

A FORMER CABINET SECRETARY 'LOOKS BACK' AT GENERAL SUNDARJI

BG Deshmukh, IAS, Cabinet Secretary through most part of the premiership of Rajiv Gandhi has, in his book titled *A Cabinet Secretary Looks Back*, provided detailed insights into the functional interplay between the Civil and Military leadership of the time. A large part of what he has elaborated relates to the then COAS, Gen K Sundarji. Deshmukh states that by the time he had assumed the appointment of Cabinet Secretary, Gen Sundarji *'had already established a commanding position in the defence field. Rajiv Gandhi was the Defence Minister and therefore all the Chiefs, especially the Army Chief General Sundarji had clear and close access to him. They (the Service Chiefs) fully exploited this proximity. To add to this, Arun Singh, the Minister of State in the Defence Ministry, was completely bowled over by the top brass. It was openly said in the Defence Ministry and outside that the Military Chief would tell what to do and he would happily fall in line. Rajiv Gandhi could not give much time to look after the running of the Ministry which was mostly left to Arun Singh to do. He therefore took many decisions, including major ones, on behalf of Rajiv Gandhi'*.[5] BG Deshmukh is unsparing of Sundarji whose tenure as Chief largely overlapped his own as Cabinet Secretary.

Attending Standing Committee Meetings

Relating an instance concerning the attendance at the Committee of Secretaries meeting, he writes that, *'the Standing Committee of Secretaries in the Cabinet Secretariat, the Core Group, met every week to discuss important security and other matters. In the first meeting held by me (BG Deshmukh), I found General Sundarji had sent his number two. I told him that next time only General Sundarji could attend and not he. The message had the desired effect but I could feel that some sort of distance had developed between us'*.[6]

Choosing a Successor

On the selection to a successor to Gen Sundarji, the books reveals that *'(Gen) Sundarji wanted to have his own nominee succeed him, to influence defence matters even after retirement. Gen Sharma being the next in seniority should have succeeded him, but Sundarji wanted a favourite General of his to step in, and it was General Nanda whom he had in mind. There was no reason not to give the job to General Sharma the post of GOC-in-C Western Command, an active command normally given to the General slated to be the Chief of Army Staff. However, this command was given to General SF Rodrigues, Vice Chief of Army Staff, who was supposed to be in the good books of General Sundarji. General Sharma was given command of the more passive Eastern Command with Headquarters in Calcutta, and General BC Nanda, junior to him, was in charge of the live Northern Command. However, the Defence Secretary noted that there was no reason to disregard General Sharma's claim. The Prime Minister agreed and Sundarji's plan fell through*'.[7]

Incident in the Ops Room

Giving details of another incident, which occurred in the Operations Room of Army Headquarters, BG Deshmukh mentions of General Sundarji having become '*rather hawkish*' and '*vigorously advocated going nuclear*'. Rajiv Gandhi, the then Prime Minister to who the Presentation was being made, listened patiently without expression on his face although his own views at that stage as known to the top bureaucrats was that he would use the nuclear option 'only as the last option'. During the meeting, BG Deshmukh writes of having asked Sundarji some questions on the payload of the nuclear head and the area that would be affected to which Sundarji curtly replied that '*Civilians need not bother about this*'. Deshmukh's retort was that he as Cabinet Secretary '*not only look after the civilian side of government but also the defence*'. This was followed, in BG Deshmukh's words by '*dead silence*' though he could see from Rajiv Gandhi's expression that he '*accepted my position*' adding that Arun Singh, however, '*looked uncomfortable*'.

Push to Technology Programmes

BG Deshmukh further mentions of General Sundarji being '*ably supported by his colleague Admiral Tahiliani, the Chief of Naval Staff. Both gave a very high profile to Indian defence. Budgetary allocations were substantially increased. The Defence Research and Development Organisation (DRDO) became highly active. India acquired the now famous Bofors gun. The Missile Programme got a big push. Work on the prototype of the Arjun Tank was given high priority. The Navy and Air Force got their share of higher allocation and greater attention. It was generally believed that all this had the personal clearance of the Prime Minister who wanted India to become a regional power*'.[8]

Relations with the Defence Secretary

On the aspect of smooth functioning of the Ministry of Defence, Deshmukh states that Sundarji's clout with the Political hierarchy '*made the position of SK Bhatnagar, the Defence Secretary, very delicate as Sundarji claimed to be senior to him and threw his weight around liberally and openly. His position in the warrant of precedence was higher and so were his emoluments. Since he was the senior most Chief of Staff who represented the whole military establishment, Sundarji would not personally attend meetings in the Defence Secretary's room and send his number two instead. Bhatnagar explained this position to me. I knew the sensitiveness of the Defence Officers and especially their Top Brass vis-à-vis civilians and their reservations about the Defence Ministry being headed by a Civilian Defence Secretary. They had always argued that the Headquarters of the military, that is Army, Navy and Air Force, should be treated as a Ministry of Government and therefore as the final authority, and resented their proposals being examined in the Defence Ministry for final orders*'.[9]

Further, that '*the intensity of tension between the Chiefs and the Defence Secretary depended upon their personalities. Bhatnagar was of mild temperament and could absorb the pressure from the Service Chiefs. But his successor, TN Seshan, was completely different. He was assertive and aggressive. The fact of being in charge of the Special Protection Group that looked after the personal security of the Prime Minister and his family gave him unrestricted access to him (the Prime Minister). The relationship between the Service Chiefs and TN Seshan became increasingly difficult, but his tenure was short one, of ten months*'.

BG Deshmukh adds that '*We heaved a sigh of relief that there had been no crisis in the Defence Ministry during this time. Seshan's successor, Naresh Chandra, was more mature and balanced. He knew how to lead a team and deal with people who had their own ego problems. During his tenure, the defence ministry functioned smoothly without giving us any anxious moments*'.

Ex Brass Tacks: Discussion in the Ops Room

There are other situations involving the Civil and Military which BG Deshmukh has written about, all of which bring out the tenuous state of Civil–Military relations. One important meeting also held in the Operations Room of Army Headquarters where General Sundarji briefed about EX BRASS TACKS, he explained,

> Pakistan was moving its armour from South in Sindh and concentrating it in the north against our Punjab border. The Army's assessment was that this was not only a tactical move but also a strategic one to threaten the Punjab. I (BG Deshmukh) asked as to why '*Pakistan should make itself vulnerable in Sindh when we had a significant presence there. There was only one major bridge over the main river and in case we bombed it, Pakistan's heavy armour would get stuck there and maybe it was removing its armour to avoid this possibility. Since we had a very strong deployment in Punjab and far superior to Pakistan's we need not worry unnecessarily about its movement of heavy armour*'.

BG Deshmukh further states that he '*was later told that (his) remarks were not taken to kindly as these were against the Army's view and also that the Army did not like a civilian, even if a Cabinet Secretary, giving a different interpretation. In fact, this massive mobilisation of the Indian Army in the guise of Army exercises on the Indo-Pak border almost led to a war between the two countries*'.

Attack on Pakistan?

The next incident BG Deshmukh mentions in his book is that of another Core Group meeting:

> *'The Secretary of RAW reported that it was openly being discussed in the Air Force messes in Punjab that India would be attacking Kapalu in Pakistan Occupied Kashmir (POK) and thereby provoking Pakistan to retaliate. I (BG Deshmukh) was upset by this information and went straight to Rajiv Gandhi. He immediately called Arun Singh and said if there was any truth in this, all these movements should be stopped at once. If this information was correct then it must have been cleared by Arun Singh but Rajiv Gandhi had obviously not been informed. An inquiry into the matter later revealed that this was a rumour floated by Pakistani Intelligence to mislead India. But this was a clever move based as it was on the well-known theories of General Sundarji, like 'coercive diplomacy' and his influence on defence matters'.*

The 'Boy' Comment

BG Deshmukh mentions about Gen Sundarji, having remarked about Rajiv Gandhi when not being allowed to escalate the situation that '***the boy has chickened out***', a remark which would have at once altered Sundarji's equation with the political hierarchy.

The Wang Dung Incident

Another example that BG Deshmukh provides to emphasise Gen Sundarji's adventurism is of the Wang Dung incident. Stating that the Indo-Chinese border was 'stable' though there was no 'formal treaty', He mentions of there being 'subsidiary intelligence Bureau outposts that *'watched the movements along the border'. The RAW also had its wireless posts to monitor communications across the border.* Deshmukh goes on to add that the Units of the Chinese Army that invaded us in 1962 were (in 1986) still deployed along the border *'as it had become a matter of prestige for that formation. It is into this no man's land that Gen Sundarji sent in strong contingent. He had justified this on grounds 'that the Chinese too had moved forward and built a strong helipad Unit'.*[10]

This being the period when Rajiv Gandhi's policy of normalising relations with China was being formulated, a warlike situation was *'not in favour'* and the steps that Gen Sundarji took were *'watched...with acute anxiety'.* In a presentation to the CCPA Meeting held at the Operations Room,, Gen Sundarji said that he had established a *'strong Indian position fully equipped to meet any threat as he did not want the Indian Army to face a similar humiliation as had happened in 1962'.*[11]

Sharp Remark

In the course of this meeting Gen Sundarji apparently made some remark about Politicians as a class by themselves. There was deadly silence thereafter and it became his (BG Deshmukh's) role to tell Gen Sundarji that 'We are a democracy and the army functions under a civilian democratic government. You should therefore be more responsible when making such remarks.'[12] *He was silent but it had to be made clear to him that 'the army had to take orders from the civilian government'.*

Field Marshal?

The former Cabinet Secretary continues his veritable tirade against General Sundarji by mentioning that '*apparently Sundarji had made up his mind to get the baton of Field Marshal and as his date of retirement neared he had many of his friends and colleagues lobbying for him. Even his wife joined in and it became rather embarrassing for all of us to avoid both of them*'.

IPKF

In regard to the IPKF, BG Deshmukh states that 'Rajiv Gandhi consulted Gen Sundarji, who, in his flamboyant style said 'If the LTTE does not agree and wants to take on the Indian Army we will finish them within a week or ten days'. As Cabinet Secretary, he set up a Committee to regularly review the situation in the light of the substantial IPKF presence. In the meetings held, 'there were rather unpleasant differences between RAW, IB and the Defence Ministry. He adds that the RAW '*now found (its) freedom of action being heavily compromised*'. About the Army, he adds that it was '*most unhappy. Gen Sundarji was personally embarrassed as the IPKF could not control and subdue the LTTE as he had promised. The Army then blamed both IB and RAW for not briefing it properly about the weaponry possessed by the LTTE or its morale and staying power*". In reply, the IB and RAW said *the Army itself was responsible because of its overconfidence and underestimation of the enemy, that is, LTTE*.'[13]

JN Dixit's Observations on The Indian Peace Keeping Force (IPKF)

In his book *Assignment Colombo* the erstwhile High Commissioner to Sri Lanka and later Foreign Secretary and NSA, JN Dixit admits that on his part he himself had 'overestimated the sincerity and political will of Jayawardane to come to a genuine compromise with the Tamils with the help of the Government of India'. However he states that on his part, the then COAS Gen K Sundarji had 'underestimated Prabhakaran's qualities of leadership and his determination to fight a prolonged war to attain the goal of Tamil Ealam'. The erstwhile Chief, when asked by Prime

Minister Rajiv Gandhi for his assessment, had given his assessment that 'once the LTTE endorsed the Agreement, they would not have the wherewithal to go back and confront India or the Sri Lankan Government'. He went on to say that 'if the LTTE decided to take on India and Sri Lanka militarily, Indian Armed Forces would be able to neutralise them militarily within two weeks'. Dixit adds that clearly 'the Army did not consider any contingency plans to be put to work in case the LTTE did not cooperate and resorted to an Armed struggle'. About the R&AW assessment, Dixit adds that it was 'very cautious' and was that 'the LTTE was not a trustworthy organisation and the Agreement in a manner, went against their high flown demand for Ealam'.[14]

Services Chiefs' Direct Access to the PM

Besides his extensive critiques of the policies and actions of General Sundarji, BG Deshmukh goes on to list some other developments pertaining to the Rajiv Gandhi era. '*During 1985-86, when Rajiv Gandhi was the Defence Minister, while the Chiefs of Staff had direct access to the Prime Minister, the latter did not have the benefit of advice of an independent Defence Minister for cross-checking. Massive amounts are involved in the purchase of defence equipment and supplies and the Prime Minister is therefore unnecessarily and personally associated with any alleged irregularity*'.

Cabinet Secretary Attends Defence Minister Meetings:

'When KC Pant became the Defence Minister, he started holding regular meetings in the Ministry to which the Cabinet Secretary was also invited, thereby sending a strong message to the Military Chiefs that the Cabinet Secretary had a vital role to play in Defence matters'. Deshmukh adds that '*the Defence Minister employed this mechanism to sort out many issues with the finance and other ministries*'.

Nuclear Policy

BG Deshmukh also sheds light on the beginnings of change to our nuclear policy. He writes of how '*hawkish our defence Chiefs were in this regard and how firmly Rajiv Gandhi resisted this pressure. At the five-nation six-continent disarmament initiative in Stockholm in early 1988, he had taken passionately argued for a world free of nuclear weapons. In July 1988, at the third Special Session on Disarmament he had stated his ambitious plan for a world free of nuclear weapons by 2010'.* In spite of this, BG Deshmukh adds, *'by end 1988 – early 1989, we were becoming acutely concerned at our vulnerability, especially when our Intelligence agencies gave us firm evidence of Pakistan having the Atomic bomb. So far we had taken only ad hoc and rudimentary steps to develop some sort of a programme that would enable us to produce atomic weapons. By now these measures seemed insufficient and inadequate in the national interest'.*[15] He then goes on to give details of how a development plan was prepared by Dr VS Arunachalam the then SA to RM and the stages of development at which specific clearances had to be taken from the Prime Minister.

On Retired Officers

At the conclusion of his very interesting Chapter on 'Economic and Defence matters', BG Deshmukh recognises that the Armed Forces being apolitical is a major reason for our remaining democratic. Moreover, he adds that *'they could have been tempted to step in when we were facing a crisis and take over the government. It may have been difficult because of the size of the country, but not impossible'.* He then stresses that *'we should not do anything to affect the base apolitical character of the Armed Forces and their professional competence and fighting qualities'.* He adds that 'there is a tendency now for retired officers to take part in politics but this cannot be interpreted as politicisation of the entire force as such' and stresses that *'we should keep in mind that Armed Forces personnel, and young officers in particular, are exposed to what is happening around them and the murky politics that is being exposed daily in the media. They are certain to have doubts about government and governance'* and cautions that *'the Authorities should keep a close watch on such developments'.*[16]

BG Deshmukh's Chapter is almost a textbook grade treatise on CMR in Indian which most issues of any importance from the Services perspective have found mention, be it the aspiration of the Services for their Headquarters being recognised as Government departments, the position of the Chiefs vis-à-vis the Defence Secretary, where he as a bureaucrat played a 'tempering' role in containing military hawkishness and emphasising the authority and responsibility of a Civilian bureaucrat to doubting or raising questions on the considered advice of the Services Chiefs.

Appointment of ACM NC Suri as CAS (1991)

Air Chief Marshal Nirmal Chandra Suri was due to retire on the same day, 31 July 1991, as his predecessor Air Chief Marshal S.K. Mehra. However, the latter obliged by demitting office in the forenoon of 31 July 1991 to enable Air Marshal Suri, handpicked by the then government, to take over as Chief in the afternoon before his retirement at the end of the day, thereby setting an entirely new precedent.

This decision had a chain effect on subsequent appointments resulting in the front runner by way of seniority, Air Marshal PK Dey being side-lined. This left Air Marshal SK Kaul as the senior most officer to succeed ACM Suri.

The Seniority Principle

Adhering to the Seniority Principle in the opinion of several senior serving and retired officers across the civil–military divide generally contributes to a turbulence free change-over. It has also been a long-standing tradition with several past cases, some mentioned above, of senior officers of yore having denied themselves appointment as Chiefs in deference to this principle.

In the wake of recent controversies involving the Service Chiefs, either when in service or after retirement, a section of Security analysts have suggested an element of merit be added onto the extant principle of seniority. Many countries, including the USA, do follow a system of deep selection. It is interesting to understand a procedure followed elsewhere to understand our own system better.

In the US system, a proviso even exists for the President to determine what is best in the national interest while making appointments. He could go beyond these officers to appoint anyone who he felt was the best suited. There have been instances where this 'overriding' proviso was invoked, as in 1970 when President Nixon picked up the 49-year-old Admiral Elmo Zumwalt, for the post of Chief of Naval Operations over 42 of his seniors. In 2003, President George Bush recalled General Peter J Schoomaker from retirement and appointed Army Chief of Staff. Though this discretion has been and intended to be used rarely, it provides the President with an 'enabling clause' that ensures there is administrative constraint in the way of appointing the 'best man for the job'.

An interesting mention in Maj Gen Shubhi Sood's book *Leadership Field Marshal Sam Manekshaw* relates to when, in April 1966 the then COAS, Gen JN Chaudhari was asked his opinion on his successor and he had sent it in writing that 'his natural successor was Gen Manekshaw'. Later that year, when Prime Minister Indira Gandhi met Sam she told him of her considering that he would be the next Chief, the latter replied that, '*Gen Kumaramangalam was senior to him and there was no way that they could make him Chief over him. The principle of seniority was the established norm in the Army and manipulation of this would not go down well with the Army. If they wanted him as Chief they would have to wait for Gen Kumaramangalam to retire*'. Gen Sood goes on to mention that '*sometime later, the Secretary to the Prime Minister met Sam in Calcutta and conveyed a message from the PM. Mr Kamaraj, who was then the President of the Congress party had met the PM and told her that if she did not appoint Gen Kumaramangalam as the next Chief, all the South Indian states would turn against her. Given this scenario, she had to concede to their request and had asked her Secretary to meet Sam and tell him how sorry she was*'.[17]

This episode also indicates to factors other than seniority and merit becoming factors in making selections for appointments to the higher ranks. To be fair to Gen Manekshaw, when the time came for him to recommend his own successor, he reinforced the principle of seniority by recommending the name of Gen PS Bhagat, though certain other circumstances had led to the seniority principle being disregarded on that occasion.

The AM–PM Theory

Air Chief Marshal OP Mehra's book *Memories Sweet and Sour* details that both General GG Bewoor and himself were to assume their appointments as Chiefs of respective Services on the same date – 15 Jan 1973. However, as decided by the Ministry of Defence, Gen GG Bewoor took over in the forenoon while he took over in the afternoon. Thus Gen Bewoor was deemed senior to him and when the Chairmanship of the COSC was to be filled at the end of the next month, it was General Bewoor who assumed the Chairmanship.

Such 'micromanagement' could only emanate from a very clear and candid understanding in the Ministry of Defence in regard to such a situation arising and their 'solution' to it. **It is unlikely that such a situation could ever have been resolved by the Services within themselves underlining the need for a 'coordinating arbiter' to administer them.**

Supersession of Vice Admiral Tony Jain (1990)

In mid-1987, CNS, Admiral R H Tahiliani of, recommended a short extension in service for Vice Admiral JG Nadkarni, the then next senior-most Naval Officer who was however otherwise due to retire in his then present rank. The obvious motive was to facilitate the latter continuing in Service till beyond his own date of retirement and enabling him to be in consideration for appointment as the next CNS. The political dispensation comprising principally Prime Minister Rajiv Gandhi, who was also Defence Minister, and the then Minister of State for Defence Arun Singh, accepted the recommendation. Vice Admiral Nadkarni was promoted to the four-star rank of Admiral and appointed CNS on 1st December 1987.

Brigadier RP Singh (Retd) and Commodore Ranjit B. Rai (Retd) in their book, *Sacked or Sunk? Admiral Vishnu Bhagwat*, detail the then CNS Admiral Tahiliani's 'desire to work out a line of succession for the Navy that would (or should) have led to the appointment of Vice Admiral Sukmal Jain (popularly known as Tony Jain) as the Navy Chief after Admiral Nadkarni's retirement to be followed next by then Rear Admiral (later Admiral) Vishnu Bhagwat".[18]

A year or so later, the Navy had its own 'supersession drama' that resulted in Vice-Admiral Tony Jain being passed over by Admiral Laxminarayan Ramdas in 1990. The build up to this alteration in the Navy's line of succession commenced as back as 1987, with the CNS obtaining an extension for Vice-Admiral J.G. Nadkarni. According to some in the Navy, a consideration for this extension being granted was that it also brought then Vice Admiral Tony Jain into the realm of consideration as the next Chief after Admiral Nadkarni.

Soon after Admiral Nadkarni took over as Chief, then Rear Admiral Vishnu Bhagwat was overlooked for appointment as Commander of the Western Fleet. What followed was somewhat unprecedented. Rear Admiral Vishnu Bhagwat was removed from reckoning for the critical post of Fleet Commander of an operational command, an appointment which is considered mandatory for an officer to be considered for the post of FOC-in-C of either of the two operational commands—the Western and Eastern Naval Commands and Rear Admiral (later Vice Admiral) Kailash K. Kohli appointed as Fleet Commander of the Western Naval Command in which Rear Admiral Vishnu Bhagwat was Chief of Staff.

Command of a Fleet being a pre-requisite for the highest ranks, this move effectively removed RADM Bhagwat from the succession chain for Navy Chief and in a somewhat questionable manner which smacked of intrigue. As the book mentions, '*Rear Admiral Kohli flew to Mumbai by a late evening flight and was driven in a car belonging to the Mazagaon Docks Limited (MDL) to the Western Naval Command headquarters where he took charge as Fleet Commander around midnight, all of which was an unprecedented manoeuvre.*'[19]

This appointment led to a major upheaval in the Navy which lasted several years. For, acting on a tip off that Rear Admiral Kohli was being appointed Fleet Commander, *Rear Admiral Vishnu Bhagwat had filed a voluminous 405 page petition in the Bombay High Court on 12th September 1990. The 13 respondents to his writ petition (number 2757) included a wide range of persons and institutions ranging from the Union of India, both the Defence and Home Ministers, the Defence Secretary, the Prime Minister's Principal Secretary at that time to eight top Navy officers beginning with the*

Navy Chief himself (Admiral Nadkarni) and his immediate senior, the FOC-in-C of the Western Naval Command Vice Admiral Jain. Incidentally, the latter too had been given a special extension until December 1990 with the ostensible aim of his being made Admiral Nadkarni's successor.

The Writ Petition had been explosive to say the least and it was for the first time that a Senior Services officer had taken the Union government, the Defence Ministry, the Prime Minister's office and virtually the entire top brass of the Navy to court for having been overlooked for an appointment and for promotion. While just the petition comprised 146 pages, the 48 annexures had run into 239 pages. As detailed by the Authors '*The allegations ranged from the petty (parties attended, overseas visits, etc. by Officers) to the more serious (professional impropriety, financial corruption, conspiracy, etc) and from the personal to the professional with the reputation of every officer named questioned. Indeed, the petition reads like the Navy was a den of debauchery, conspiracy, degeneration, anti-national activities and corruption which would put Nero to shame.*'[20]

Eventually, the writ petition resulted in a compromise. Rear Admiral Bhagwat withdrew his petition and was subsequently appointed Fleet Commander of the Eastern Naval Command. The reason(s) for the compromise is a subject of much debate and speculation. Whatever the reason, the compromise was arguably a questionable way out. The charges against the officers were never proved or disproved and yet their reputation was maligned. The original planned succession chain, however, did not work. *After this rather bitter experience of RADM Bhagwat's Writ Petition, the Government was guarded in its approach and not inclined to accede to one more case of an officer being granted an extension being made eligible for appointment as CNS. This had a salutary effect as there is no other subsequent case of grant of extensions at the highest levels. Vice-Admiral Tony Jain was thereafter superseded and his junior Admiral Laxminarayan Ramdas appointed as CNS in succession to Admiral Nadkarni.*

Interestingly, Vice Admiral Jain's supersession and Vice Admiral Ramdas' appointment was decided before Prime Minister VP Singh (who was also Defence Minister) resigned on 10th November 1990, before the date the latter was to assume the higher rank. When Shri Chandrashekhar took over as Prime Minister that same day, there were still 21 days for Vice Admiral Ramdas to formally take charge as CNS and had soon after taking charge considered reversing his predecessor's decision and giving Admiral Nadkarni extension for a month in order to consider someone else (possibly Vice Admiral Jain) for the Navy's top post.

The former President of India, Shri R Venkataraman in his book *My Presidential Years,* mentions that soon after the Government under the Prime Ministership of Shri Chandrashekhar assumed office, overtures were made to the Office of the President as to whether the appointment of VADM Ramdas as CNS could be rescinded. The President conveyed reluctance as the orders of succession had already been issued. It was then suggested from the side of the Prime Minister as to whether Admiral Nadkarni could be given an extension. As President, he again did not budge on grounds that there was no obvious rationale for such an extraordinary step and in his view, a Service Chief on extension would fail to command the unequivocal allegiance of his men, besides setting a 'bad precedent'.

The Rodrigues Interview (1992)

On 20 February 1992, a request was received by the MA to COAS from the Directorate of Public Relations, Ministry of Defence, for an interview being granted by the COAS to Ramindar Singh, Senior Editor of the Lucknow daily *The Pioneer.* The interview was conducted on 04 March and published on 11 & 12 March 1992. The acclaimed political analyst (Late) Vinod Mehta was then the newspaper's Editor-in-Chief. Gen SF Rodrigues, the then COAS was reluctant to grant the interview but the same was incessantly pressed by Col PN Khera, the then PRO (Army) in the Public Relations Department of the Ministry of Defence who pleaded before Brigadier (later Major General) SK Kariappa that the correspondent was 'like his younger brother' and the interview would benefit his own fledgling career. Ramindar Singh sought permission to tape-record the interview which too graciously and trustingly accorded on the assurance that the final text should be forwarded for 'vetting' the intended responses. Gen Rodrigues agreed to the requests but on condition that it be conveyed to the correspondent that the script of the

Interview be sent for perusal prior to its publication. Ramindar Singh gave a 'gentleman's promise' to do so but subsequently reneged on it.

Read carefully, there was no willful intent on the part of Gen Rodrigues to 'criticize' the Government. What he wished to emphasise that with prolonged involvement of the Army in maintenance of law and order, its ability to perform the core function of safeguarding borders does get impacted. It was, however, in the choice of phrases and words that offended parliamentarians. One was his referring to some politicians as 'bandicoots' and another, a rather controversial statement in the context of CMR, that (for the Armed Forces) 'good governance is also our concern'. Though not elaborated by the General, the apparent reference had been to the law and order situation in some States of the country where the Army had been called out to restore or maintain peace. The General had obviously spoken freely and trustingly, with his usual geniality, informality and warmth.

Gen Rodrigues was away on an official visit to Nepal on the day the interview appeared in *The Pioneer*. Many in fact think this was so timed with due deliberation. There was little 'damage control' Gen Rodrigues could have done and by the time he returned, the interview caused a storm that raged even in the Parliament.

It was only later transpired that the entire interview episode was a devious and well-strategized 'set up' with the silent collusion on the part of some officials in the Ministry of Defence. The episode climaxed with a statement on the floor of Parliament by the then Defence Minister Sharad Pawar which mentioned inter alia, '*I have discussed the matter with the General and find that while certain impression has been created, he made it abundantly clear to me that he stands fully committed to follow Government's policy and directions in regard to each of the various issues referred in his interview. I am satisfied with the General's explanation. However, I feel that such interviews by serving officer are best avoided. I wish he had resisted the temptation.*' The Statement, tantamount to an admonishment of Gen Rodrigues, who now had the option of either resigning with dignity or accepting the reprimand. To the disappointment of several of his colleagues and juniors, he chose the latter option resulting in a much lowered stature of the Chiefs in relation to the Ministry of Defence.

The 'Civil Military' issues involved in this episode are firstly, whether the Ministry of Defence was complicit in 'setting up' this interview. The preponderant belief in the Service is 'Yes' and the role of the then PRO (Army) being regarded as most suspect, in fact of being the perpetrator. Second, when the request itself had come from the Ministry of Defence, to admonish the Chief for not 'resisting to a temptation' would not be fair as he did not solicit the interview at all. Even though reluctant to grant the interview, it was a Ministry of Defence official who persuaded him to grant it.

The second was whether the whole matter could have been better handled both administratively as also on the floor of the House and the Chief provided a window to 'save grace'. Many felt that should have been done. *One recurrent argument has been that national purpose is served by belittling or denigrating a Chief before the eyes of his troops. He is the eventual fountainhead for all directions and orders and his stature being lowered only dilutes the efficacy of the force of these orders. If there are situations where the course of actions or conduct of a Service Chief needs to be corrected, the same should be effected in silent discretion rather than make a public spectacle of both the Chief and the System.*

K Subrahmanyam, in an Article 'Educating the Forces' carried in the *Business and Political Observer* of 23 March 1992 emphasised that while the remarks in the interview on the Army's stake in good governance was interpreted as criticism of the Government, but read in the context of deployment of the Army deployment in Punjab, J&K and Assam, could well have an honest and unimpeachable import. Unlike in other advanced democracies, the Government of India does not come out with policy documents setting out threat assessments and the Government's strategy to deal with them. If such documents are available on defence as well as other areas, including our nuclear policy, the kind of predicament of the Army Chief giving an assessment perhaps not wholly in consonance with that of the Government's would not have arisen.

In conclusion to the article, Shri Subrahmanyam adds that '*none of us can afford to neglect thinking and caring about good governance*' and pushes the point further by adding that this '*appears to be the last thing worrying our parliamentarians and ministers*' emphasising that '*good governance would start with an orderly and decorous parliament willing to listen and learn*'.

The former CNS, Admiral JG Nadkarni writing in the same paper wrote '*India is more likely to produce a soldier-sycophant rather than a soldier statesman*'.

Admiral Bhagwat's Dismissal (1998)

The nadir of CMR in post-independence India was touched with the dismissal of the then Chief of the Naval Staff, Admiral Vishnu Bhagwat. The 'proximate cause' of the dismissal was the Government's decision to appoint Vice Admiral Harinder Singh, then FOC A&N, as the Deputy Chief of Naval Staff against the recommendations of Admiral Bhagwat. The dismissal itself became an inevitability after the CNS took an uncompromising stance publicly terming the posting as 'unimplementable'.

From a Civil–Military standpoint, what is significant is that there was no attempt on the part of the government to pacify the CNS or to address his concerns. There was a degree of personal animosity between VADM Harinder Singh and the Bhagwats and it would anyway have been unlikely that as DCNS (who controls the operational aspects of the Navy) would have been conducive, a factor that the Government would not have been missed. Admiral Bhagwat, was not given any face-saving escape route leading many to believe at that time that the causative factors for his dismissal lay in reasons beyond his intransigence.

The immediate stated reason for Admiral Bhagwat's dismissal was his staunch and uncompromising defiance to execute the decision of the Government (approved by the ACC) appointing Vice-Admiral Harinder Singh, the then Fortress Commander in the Andaman and Nicobar Islands, as DCNS. This decision of the ACC was conveyed to the naval HQ for implementation on 09 December 1998. The very next day,

Admiral Bhagwat forwarded to the then Home Minister L.K. Advani, transcripts of the recordings of telephone conversations between VADM Harinder Singh and some other FOC-in-C level officers, which had been recorded by VADM Harinder Singh and forwarded to the editor of the *Punjab Kesari* and contained mention by those senior officers that the CNS' obstruction to his promotion was due to personal animosity.

The CNS desired the Home Ministry to prosecute VADM Harinder Singh for unauthorised recording of the conversations. In his conversation with Shri Advani, Admiral Bhagwat apparently conveyed that he would rather be dismissed than accept an officer who was so recalcitrant, as his DCNS. On Shri Advani's suggestion, Admiral Bhagwat met and explained the issue to the then President of India Shri KR Narayanan. He also formally raised the issue with the Defence Minister George Fernandes emphasising that he, as CNS 'must have implicit trust and confidence' and that on his part, VADM Harinder Singh's conduct had 'violated all norms of good order and naval discipline'. The Defence Ministry's order of December 9 was therefore 'unimplementable', being in violation of Regulation 134 of the Navy Act, which stipulated that 'the Government shall make appointments of Captain and above on the recommendation' of the CNS.

In support of his stance, Admiral Bhagwat relied on an affidavit submitted by the Government in their response to a Writ petition filed by Lieutenant-General RS Kadyan, challenging the appointment of Lt-Gen H.R.S. Kalkat as GOC-in-C Eastern Command in which the Government had elaborated the procedure followed as the selection for Army Commanders according to which The Chief of the Army Staff would assess merit and suitability of eligible officers to make his recommendations. The underlying primacy in this procedure was understood to be that Merit and suitability being at par, due consideration is given to the seniority of an officer. However, merit and suitability are not to be compromised for the sake of seniority.

Also interesting are the grounds for Admiral Bhagwat's animosity. Admiral Bhagwat alleged that VADM Harinder Singh had 'incited communalism in the Armed Forces' by attempting to 'alienate officers of the Sikh community', he called the CNS' wife Niloufer Bhagwat a half-

Muslim' and a CPI 'Card Holder' and of being the Party's lawyer before the Srikrishna Commission of Inquiry. On her part, Mrs Nilofer Bhagwat had also written directly to the Raksha Mantri about VADM Harinder Singh. The latter in fact also made an allegation against Lt. Cdr. A.A. Lone, the only Kashmiri Muslim Officer in the navy at the time and questioned his patriotism by alleging links with a person involved in hawala transactions for arms for Kashmir terrorists When called to account for these misdemeanours, he had supposedly tendered an 'unqualified apology' addressed to the Ministry of Defence who in turn informed Naval Headquarters (NHQ) of its receipt of this apology but did not share it with either the CNS or any other officers who VADM Harinder Singh had spoken against. There were also doubts on VADM Harinder Singh's probity. In subsequent developments, the then Raksha Mantri George Fernandes revealed that Admiral Bhagwat had, in irritation at a statutory complaint filed by Vice-Admiral Sushil Kumar, later appointed as his successor, even threatened to court-martial him. This has, however, never been corroborated.

On 28 December the CNS clarified that the ACC decision being 'unimplementable' was on the justification that 'since the ACC had arrived at it on the basis of insufficient information about the officer's service record'. This argument obviously did not find favour with the Government who on 30 December 1998 unceremoniously dismissed Admiral Bhagwat.

Parallel to these developments, there was a running discord between the three Service Chiefs and the Defence Secretary Shri Ajit Kumar which assumed such proportions as requiring the three Chiefs to jointly address a communication to the Raksha Mantri protesting the Defence Secretary's 'negativism'.

The above facts are adequate to surmise the state discord between the Ministry of Defence and the Services Headquarters. The extent of the personality play involved is also obvious and this becomes a reason for departure from exercising a principled 'command and control' by the Ministry based on addressing issues rather than a broad sweep neglect in addressing matters raised by the Services Chiefs themselves.

It needs emphasis that there is no level of authority beyond them to put forward the case of the Services and unless there is a functional system in place which provides reasoned arguments for specific Government decisions, the interplay between individuals would continue to have a deleterious effect on the effective and efficient administration of the Services.

An interesting episode pertaining just prior to the dismissal was the effort by Shri Sharad Pawar, then Leader of the Opposition in the Lok Sabha and a former Defence Minister who took up the matter with both the Prime and Defence Ministers. In a forceful letter Pawar drew attention to the large number of Petitions pending in various Courts that related to VADM Harinder Singh and wrote that '*...one of my observations as Raksha Mantri was that, the Armed Forces were not tainted by the divisive forces which are currently at work in our country. My experience was that the Armed Forces were 'Indian' and were not concerned with religious, political or communal ideology except at very peripheral level. I believe that this is one of the greatest strengths of the country. It would be disastrous to allow anybody or anything to shake this*'.

General Padmanabhan chided as 'Cavalier'

During the traditional COAS' 'Army Day' media interaction in 2002, which took place in the midst of the mobilisation of the Armed Forces, the then COAS Gen Padmanabhan responded to a pointed question on the possible use of nuclear weapons by the enemy with a forthright candid response that caused a national stir and evoked a response from neighbouring country. Though the statement was in keeping with the national nuclear doctrine of the time and that the Defence Minister himself had recently articulated the same opinion, the latter publicly 'chided' General Padmanabhan by calling his response as being 'cavalier'. It was later explained and even conveyed to the Chief that the Defence Minister's intervention was made to 'calm temperatures' raised on account of the Statement. **The CMR issue here is that military ethos does not permit even ticking off an appointment holder in the presence of his command. The political class at times and quite certainly in this case, completely missed this sensitive feature of military ethos.**

Issues Impinging on Senior Officer Management

There have been a few long-standing suggestions made regarding the management of promotions and appointments at senior ranks by the Ministry of Defence that merit mention:

(a) **Date of Birth:** The importance attached to the date of birth and seniority in service determined at the time of the commission into service. A proposal for inter se seniority amongst officers of a batch being re-fixed at the stage of promotion to the rank of Brigadier and equivalent is regularly mooted and then dropped from being pursued.

(b) **Residual Service Clause:** Of the officers promoted to the rank of Lt-Gen, only those who have at least three years of residual service get to command corps even though the normal tenure of Corps Commanders is just about one year. And among Corps Commanders, only those who have at least two years residual service make it to Army Commander. As long as an officer approved for promotion has adequate residual tenure to command a corps, this should be considered suffice.

(c) **Eligibility for Promotion:** Presently, only those officers who have commanded Corps are considered for promotion as Army Commanders. They are 'reported upon' and hence their promotion is based on the strength of their performance. However, there is no 'reporting' on Army Commanders and hence for promotion to as Service Chiefs, it is the very same record up to and including command of a Corps that is considered along with a recommendation of the Chief of the Army Staff. Other than this input, it is notes recorded in the MoD, and inputs from Agencies such as the Intelligence Bureau (IB) which matter in the final decision. But, the IB cannot as such report on the professional capability of the selectees. Their focus is more on personal conduct. (Former IB Director, BN Mullick's case of having scuttling the prospects of Gen SPP Thorat being considered for the Army Chief as successor to General Thimayya is legend). There is a proposal to allow direct interaction of Army Commanders with the political leadership.

SOME 'MENTIONABLE' INCIDENTS

On Awards

Lt Gen Harbaksh Singh in his book has written of how he '*sought an interview with the Defence minister, Mr Chavan, to discuss the matter (about awards). I made it quite clear to him that General Chaudhuri had not taken any part in the fighting and did not deserve to be awarded a Padma Vibhushan. He told me that his case for the award was only of symbolic value; and tried to mollify me by saying that the Government of India was considering me for a special award, and, besides had decided to give me the rank of a full general. Mr Lal Bahadur Shastri, the then Prime Minister, died in Tashkent...so nothing came of the special awards that I had been promised though I was given the Padma Vibhushan after retirement*'.[21]

This incident, more in the nature of an admission somewhat agitates against the spirit of camaraderie for which the Services are known. It also reveals how awards are 'clamoured for' and gives a peek into the very thinly veiled secret that selection for higher awards has been an instrument of control over the Services that has been used to good effect. The cases in recent past of Services personnel being bestowed 'Padma' series of awards are these days few and far between.[22]

Concerns on ACM OP Mehra's Health

ACM OP Mehra's Autobiography *Of Memories Sweet and Sour* mentions an episode of pertinence to the nature of Civilian[23] control over the Military leadership. According to Mehra, a few months after he had taken over, he felt uneasy during his morning walk and was advised some checkups and admission to hospital. While he underwent the tests that revealed his having ischemic heart disease, but he was not prepared for admission. Instead he chose to rest at home. The hospital on its part stationed a qualified cardiologist at his residence to carry out the frequent tests and be available in case of an emergency.

Several rumours about his health began to quickly do the rounds which reached the then Raksha Mantri Babu Jagjivan Ram who remarked that '*If the man is sick, how can he perform the duties as head of the service?*'.

As it happened, during the period of his being unwell, a meeting of the DRDO and DPSUs had been called by the then RRM Shri VC Shukla. As he (ACM Mehra) held dual charge as Chairman HAL at that time, he requested the RRM to attend the meeting which received media coverage with photographs published of the with other attendees.

It later transpired that Babu Jagjivan Ram had raised the issue of his health with the Prime Minister Smt Indira Gandhi who having seen the photographs of the meeting responded by asking as to how, if he was not fit to carry out his duties, was he attending such a meeting. The matter was thereafter closed.

General TN Raina's Principled Stand

An occasion where a Service Chief had reportedly taken an extraordinary principled stand deserves mention. Apurba Kundu a scholar on CMR and author of *Militarism in India* quotes from an interview granted by an erstwhile Adjutant General who mentioned that just before declaring Emergency, that Prime Minister Smt Indira Gandhi had summoned the then Chief of Army Staff and 'put him in the picture'. General Raina reportedly told Mrs Gandhi *'very bluntly'* that the Army would not be used to *'further her ends' but obey only those orders of 'a legally construed government'.* This is still widely acclaimed in Army circles to be a defining stand that led to 'keeping the military out of Politics' during his tenure and has obviously served as guiding principle to successor Chiefs of Staff.

ACM Latif 'scares' the Prime Minister

In her biography of her husband titled *The Ladder of his Life – Biography of Air Chief Marshal Idris Hasan Latif, PVSM*, Bilkees Latif has recounted details of an incidence where a presentation was to be given to the Prime Minister at the Air Headquarters on the induction of deep penetration strike aircraft. In ACM Latif's *words 'I decided on a short presentation concentrated on a graphic comparison of our strike capability with that of our immediate adversary, the main thrust being on the relative 'throw weights' and radii of action of the strike aircraft of the two Air Forces involved. After the briefing, escorting him to the lift, he looked at me with his rather charming smile and said to me in Hindi, "Mujhe daraate ho?" "If the facts are frightening, Sir," I replied, "remedial measures are clearly overdue".*'[24] ACM Latif adds that soon afterwards, the Prime Minister called for another meeting and directed him (CAS), the Defence Secretary and other Officers to proceed to UK to finalise the deal.

Prime Minister Deve Gowda's Tirade

In April 1999, former Prime Minster HD Deve Gowda, in the course of his address to parliament on the Confidence vote for his Government launched a veritable tirade against a serving Deputy Chief of Army Staff. *The then Army Chief, General VP Malik not only brought the incident to the notice of the President of India to both, defend the honour of the otherwise excellent officer but also reiterated the apolitical character of the Army. Equally, he pushed hard to ensure that the then Defence Minister write to the Speaker and apprise him of the impeccable credentials of the officer concerned, urging for the remarks being expunged.*

Sachar Committee

Mention was on the part of the Services to the requirement of the Sachar Committee that was set up in March 2005 to ascertain inter alia the presence and participation of Muslims in the Government structure with a view to consider policies and reforms for elevating the status of minorities in the country. Apart from the Government, its brief is to also survey the socio-economic conditions of Muslims in the armed forces. When the requirement for details was projected to the Army Headquarters, the then COAS, Gen JJ Singh refused to provide the 'headcount' by emphasising that *"all Indians get a fair chance of joining the Armed Forces"* and that the Armed Forces "*take great pride in their ability to keep their heads far above communal waters*". This response of Gen Singh very strongly underlined the secular and apolitical nature of the Armed Forces.

The Navy and Air Force had, however, supplied the information to the Government. The Army's stand was vindicated when the then Raksha Mantri AK Antony endorsed their viewpoint and the information required was neither collated not provided. As the request for information for providing the data sought had come through the Ministry of Defence, this issue was mentioned to stress upon the lack of sensitivity to and understanding of the core ethics and ethos of the Defence Services in the Ministry of Defence.

Jaswant Singh's Caustic Remarks on a Service COAS

An important aspect of Civilian Control over the Military arose when, in February 2008, in the course of a discussion on the floor of the Rajya Sabha, Jaswant Singh, a Cabinet Minister then in the Opposition referred to a statement of the then COAS in the course of a television interview my mentioning *"very recently, and repeatedly, some most unwanted, unwise, and also, if I may say so, irresponsible and therefore unacceptable statements were made by the Chief of the Army staff on television.... the Chief of the Army Staff is certainly not the authority to comment or rule on the importance of encroachments on the border and what the response ought to be...It is unbecoming, unwanted and irresponsible and it is harmful for the dignity not just of the high office that he holds but also for the total responsibility that he carries and for the security of the country"*.[25]

The issues which arose were firstly, the qualifications of the COAS to mention a fact or opinion on a matter of national concern is never in doubt. Even if he had exceeded his brief, so to speak, was there need to belittle an Army Chief on the floor of Parliament without having given him an opportunity to justify his remarks. This incident, more because the denigrating statement came from and MP who was an erstwhile Service officer, had caused considerable concern in Service circles.

SOME RECENT ISSUES

There are some recent issues on which there are varied opinions upon merits or otherwise on both sides of the civil and military divide but which have not helped the two sides to get closer. Being of recent vintage, these issues still come up for frequent discussions and reference and facts relating to these are fresh in discerning minds with opinions on these being encrusted. As the din and dust on these have yet to settle, reference to these is limited to the purport of this book with the opportunity for any further incisive examination left for posterity.

Gen VK Singh Date of Birth Issue

From the perspective of CMR watchers, there were certain 'firsts' that came to fore from the various aspects of this issue. The foremost of these is the fact that a serving Chief of Staff submitted a statutory complaint to redress a grievance. In doing so, he invoked Section 27 of the Army Act, a provision available to all serving personnel. The grievance being of a nature that only the authority appealed to the 'Central Government' could have redressed, invoking this provision, even if by a serving Chief of Staff, is procedurally correct. The second aspect is that of a serving Chief of Staff approaching the Hon'ble Supreme Court of India against the 'rejection' of his complaint by the Government. Bereft of considerations such as 'precedence' and 'service ethos' The General's entitlement to approach the Courts of the land are not curtailed in any way by his tenanting a 'high office'.

The manner in which the entire 'Date of Birth' issue of the former COAS was addressed has set a 'precedence', if ever required in future, to serve as the template to address such a case in future. Posterity would no doubt revisit this issue to examine it in greater depth and focus on the dynamics of how the then Government 'handled' the issue, particularly whether the episode was allowed to spin-tail as a confrontation between the Government and its Army Chief. As the 'higher authority' it was incumbent on Government to raise above and adopt a holistic consideration. The argument on the side of the bureaucrats has been that the 'situation' was brought upon by the Chief himself. The 'Services' response to that view is that there is no single point during that entire 'episode' where the Chief had stepped out of the rule book and it is the discomfiture, inexperience and insecurity of the bureaucrats to deal with Service Chief having a mind of his own that lay at the root of the issue.

Admiral DK Joshi's Resignation

Admiral DK Joshi, who assumed charge as Chief of the Naval Staff on 31 Aug 2012 was due to retire on superannuation in the normal course only on Aug 2015. The Admiral, however, resigned from service on 26 February 2014, taking moral responsibility for an accident on board the submarine INS Sindhuratna in which two officers were killed after one of the submarine's compartments was filled with smoke during a sea trial. This accident followed a few other accidents that took place on its other submarines and ships that raised doubts on the safety record of the Indian Navy.

The then Defence Minister Shri AK Antony had reportedly summoned Admiral Joshi to seek an explanation for the Sindhuratna mishap in the course of which meeting, the Admiral is believed to have accepted moral responsibility and offered to resign. Soon after the meeting on the very day, Shri AK Antony met both the Prime Minister and the President to apprise them and the Admiral's resignation which was accepted that very evening.

There is a general acceptance in amongst officers of the Navy that Admiral DK Joshi, was a '*hard taskmaster*' who '*always ran tight ships*'. He was '*unforgiving*' as a Commanding Officer and that by resigning he had '*lived up to his own exacting standards*'.

The issue left for posterity is therefore whether such an offer of resignation should indeed have been accepted, the 'haste' with which this was done with no apparent attempt or effort to assuage or 'calm down' any tempest that may have raged during the meeting. Two aspects emphasised by former Navy Officers are first, that there was no personal culpability on the part of the Admiral. Reportedly, an official investigation into the incident had found that deaths occurred due to failure to adhere to mandatory protocols to wear gas masks. The second, and somewhat ominous aspect from the CMR perspective is of the 'resignation', not having made as per laid down procedure had initially been equated with desertion for purposes of assessing the Admiral's post-service entitlements. It was only after several months that he received his post-retirement benefits and entitlements which were regularised as a 'special case'.

An insight into the conflict comes from Admiral Joshi's observations made to a media channel that the functional arrangement (between the Ministry of Defence and the Services) was one, in his words, '*Where there is authority, there is no accountability and where there is responsibility, the authority is not there*'. The root cause, Admiral Joshi stresses, was the 'dysfunctional and inefficient' business model that exists wherein professional competence, domain expertise, accountability, responsibility and authority, these all reside in separate silos in different locations. He observes that 'whilst professional competence, domain expertise, accountability, responsibility is with the service, that is not the case with the authority' to stress that 'higher management of defence needs reforms'.

A further issue in the entire episode had been that in appointing the successor to Admiral Joshi, the next senior-most officer, VADM Shekhar Sinha had been overlooked. The Bureaucrats argument for this is straightforward – as the FOC-in-C of the Command in which the INS Sindhuratna and some other preceding incidents had taken place, his direct responsibility over the fleet was even more than that of the CNS. Appointing him CNS would tantamount to 'rewarding' him for the same causes that compelled his Chief to submit his resignation. VADM Sinha chose to also submit his application for premature retirement which was duly accepted.

Political Work versus Ministerial Responsibilities

Several Military officials as also a few from the Civil Services have mentioned of successive Defence Ministers from George Fernandes to Pranab Mukherjee and AK Antony chairing or being members of various political committees of their respective political parties and of their immense experience and political skills being utilised to obtain consensus on contentious issues. While George Fernandes and Pranab Mukherjee both kept long hours and ensured that adequate time was invariably slotted for Defence Ministry work, there is a grouse expressed that notwithstanding his sharp and incisive understanding and relatively speedy clearing files, Shri Antony had far too many political responsibilities placed on his shoulders which gave him little time to hear out the viewpoint of the Services. Resultantly, he relied heavily on the advice and opinion of the bureaucracy whose version overwhelmingly prevailed. The present phase, with a Defence Minister less encumbered with other political responsibilities and with a full-time 'hands on' approach to his work has been mentioned by one senior officer as a 'sunshine period'.

NOTES

1. Singh, Depinder, op. cit., p. 207.
2. 'In the Service of the Nation – Reminiscences' by General KV Krishna Rao (Penguin Books India Ltd, 2001), p. 245.
3. 'In the Service of the Nation – Reminisences' by General KV Krishna Rao (Penguin Books India Ltd, 2001), p. 246.
4. Lt Gen Sinha, S.K., *A Soldier Recalls* (New Delhi: Lancer International, 1992), p. 298.
5. Deshmukh, B.G., *From Poona to Prime Minister's Office – A Cabinet Secretary looks back*, Harper Collins.
6. Ibid., p. 164
7. Ibid., p. 166.
8. Deshmukh, op. cit., p. 163.
9. Deshmukh, op. cit., p. 164.
10. Deshmukh, op. cit., p. 166.
11. Deshmukh, op. cit., p. 165.
12. Deshmukh, op. cit., p. 168.
13. Deshmukh, op. cit., p. 168.
14. Dixit, J.N., *Assignment Colombo* (Delhi: Konark Publishers, 1997), p. 416.
15. Deshmukh, op. cit., p. 171.
16. Deshmukh, op. cit., p. 172.
17. Maj. Gen. Sood, Shubhi, *Leadership Field Marshal Sam Manekshaw* (Noida: SDS Publishers, 2006), pp. 43-44.
18. Brig Singh, R.P. and Cmde Rai, Ranjit B., *Sacked or Sunk? Admiral Vishnu Bhagwat* (New Delhi: Manas Publications, 2000), p. 120.
19. Singh and Rai, op. cit., p. 124.
20. Singh and Rai, op. cit., p. 134.
21. Lt. Gen Singh, Harbaksh, *War Despatches*, Lancer Publications.
22. Ibid.
23. Air Chief Marshal Mehra, O.P. Mehra, *Memories Sweet and Sour*, KW Publishers, 2010.
24. Latif, Bilkees, *The Ladder of his Life – Biography of Air Chief Marshal Idris Hasan Latif, PVSM* (New Delhi: KW Publishers), 2013.
25. Rajya Sabha Proceedings, 26 February 2008.

CHAPTER 7

'REFORM' COMMITTEES

THE EXPERT COMMITTEE ON DEFENCE PLANNING 1978

Gen KV Krishna Rao's autobiography *In the Service of the Nation* gives an insight into the constitution of an Expert Committee on Defence Planning which had been chaired by him. Gen Rao states:

> Govind Narain, the (then) Defence Secretary initiated the case bringing out the changing scenario, the need for the requisite defence preparedness to maintain credibility in the world, the escalating defence budget, the greater sophistication in weapons and equipment, the concurrent increase in manpower costs, the ad hoc manner in which matters were dealt with, and the need for ensuring maximum possible cost effectiveness while endeavouring to improve the fighting capacity of the defence forces. He recommended that a high level Expert Committee be constituted to examine the whole position in depth and to suggest in detail measures required for the for the future build up of necessary defence.

The Committee Report

The Report of the Committee, Gen Rao states '...*covered all the important aspects of defence preparedness, including, besides threats to national vital interests, future strategy, force levels over different time frames, future battle field environment, acquisition and production of sophisticated equipment, improvement in command and control, as also of intelligence, and measures to redeploy resources for improved and more cost effective utilisation*'.[1]

The Report's recommendations when implemented would result in '*considerable improvement in the teeth-to-tail ratio, and ultimate attainment of a reasonable deterrence capability. About one lakh personnel and about 20,000 vehicles of all types was found from within the resources of the Army, and in the process, a saving of Rs 200 Crores initial and Rs 100 Crores recurring expenditure*', which Gen Rao mentions '*most of which would be ploughed back into modernisation measures*'. He adds that '*basically, the thrust of the recommendations was towards enhancing fire power, mobility, night fighting capability, electronic warfare capability, and so on and thus developing adequate deterrence capability*'.

Subsequent to completing command of his Corps, Gen KV Krishna Rao was posted as Deputy Chief of Army Staff. He realised upon taking over the appointment that 'the processing of the Expert Committee Report within the Army itself left much to be desired. Instead of concentrating on the macro issues such as threat and the force levels, and organisation of major formations, the Army got involved in comparatively minor aspects'. Further, although a copy of the Report had been forwarded to the Defence Secretary on 30 October 1976, the Army Headquarters recommendations were only sent on 04 March 1978, a fortnight before (Gen Rao's) taking over as Deputy Chief.

This was the time when the Defence Five Year Plan (1979–84) was also under formulation. Gen Rao states that '*as far as that was concerned, a plan of sorts was made but the justification given for various recommendations was not convincing enough, nor were the Committee's recommendations adequately reflected. While some of these should have been got through in the 1974–79 Plan itself, at least in the 1979–84, plan advantage should have been taken of it being a Government Committee to include the important and more compelling recommendations*'.

How the Report was progressed at Army HQ and the Ministry of Defence

Providing details of the dynamics of how this situation evolved thereafter, Gen Rao mentions that though "*the Expert Committee envisaged a saving of over a lakh personnel, the deliberations at Army Headquarters could only effect marginal savings of about 10,000 personnel. Thus, when Army Plan 1979–84 was projected separately and a commitment of savings of over one lakh personnel for new raisings was indicated to the government, the government insisted that the Army fulfil the commitment before any new measures could be agreed to. Army Headquarters was in a quandary and the government would not budge".*

Another aspect of this 'standoff' which Gen Rao mentions is that '***the government took objection to a remark in the covering note of the Expert Committee Report, to the effect that directions on implementation of some of the recommendations of the Committee had been issued by Army Headquarters, on the plea that these had considerable policy and financial implications. Both the Army Plan as well as the implementation of the Expert Committee recommendations were, therefore, held up***'.[2]

Gen Rao's Dilemma

On how the 'standoff' with the government was resolved, Gen Rao took up the matter with the Defence Secretary, who was given as thorough briefing on the Expert Committee Report followed by a discussion on the Army Plan and explained the changes necessary in the light of the Report.

The Defence Secretary thereupon discussed the Plan with the Defence Minister and even shared the note he put up to the Defence Minister with him (Gen Rao) and a case taken up with the Cabinet Committee for Political Affairs (CCPA) whereupon 'a Committee for Defence Planning (CDP) was constituted by the Government in July 1978 headed by the Cabinet Secretary.

The insights Gen Rao has provided on the deliberations at the CDP Meetings are interesting. He states that *'often, during discussions, the finance and planning secretaries would oppose the major proposals, due to inadequate understanding of defence. They would question such aspects as threat perception, the force levels and other such operational matters, without advancing any convincing counter-arguments themselves'.*

Identifying a major structural problem, Gen Rao states that '*we found that the main problem was that finance was not integrated with defence, as far as the Defence Ministry was concerned*'.[3] He summarises the net effect of the CCPA approvals to be the teeth-to-tail ratio improving to 70:30 and the amount spent on modernisation going up from 3 to 20 percent. Gen Rao adds *that 'strangely we found that even after approval by the CCPA of various schemes, finance would question these and seek re-examination, thus causing considerable delay in the implementation of vital measures*'. He adds that a case had therefore to be taken up for streamlining financial procedures to ensure that the plan approved by the CCPA was implemented effectively.

As a lesson learnt in dealing with the Ministry, Gen Rao's observation is that overall '*trying to get cases through in a piecemeal fashion, which was the prevailing practice, would not benefit the service in the long run. The Ministries concerned see through the game and block cases in due course. On the other hand, comprehensive cases, fully supported with convincing reasons stood a better chance of going through. I also found that close and intimate rapport and thorough briefing of the highest officials at the Secretary level helped a lot in the successful finalisation of our cases*'.[4]

There are, however, two aspects of the Committee on Defence Planning that merit mention. First, there was no political executive or leadership to the Committee. The Service Chiefs did not get a direct interface with any Political Authority. The second aspect, significant in terms of protocol was that for the first time after the Defence Secretary's Committees were subsumed into the Defence Ministers Committees that the Service Chiefs were nominated as members of a Committee headed by a Civil Servant. This needs to be borne in mind when understanding the interactions of BG Deshmukh and Gen K Sundarji (also detailed in this Report).

Creation of the Appointment of DG DPS

In 1986, an Inter-Services organisation called Directorate General Defence Planning Staff was created to provide support to the Chiefs of Staff Committee. It was unique in its composition as besides representatives from the three Services, it included representatives from the Ministry of External affairs and the Defence Research and Development Organisation and had a wide-ranging mandate including the following main subjects:

(a) Threat analysis and formulation of threats assessments
(b) The evolution of Military aims
(c) Formulation of the concept of combined operations
(d) Conception and recommendations (to COSC) regarding balanced force levels to achieve military aims.
(e) Joint training and joint logistic management
(f) Coordination of Perspective plans for 15-20 year period.
(g) Maintain close interaction with R&D, Defence Production Industry and Finance.

Being an organisation set up in support of the COSC, how it served its purpose depended on the directions received from the COSC or higher authorities. Functionally, its efficiency was hamstrung by lack of coordination between the three Services towards various issues. The original proposal to set up the DG DPS organisation was for it to be a Strategic Planning Committee headed by the Defence Minister with the Minister of State, Service Chiefs, Defence Secretary, Financial Adviser and the Director IDSA as its members, which would have given a role in the policy formulation apparatus of the Ministry of Defence. As this was not implemented and the DG DPS given a role as a support organisation to the COSC, its originally intended role did not materialise.

COMMITTEE ON DEFENCE EXPENDITURE (CDE)

Arun Singh, who had been the Raksha Rajya Mantri in the cabinet of Rajiv Gandhi, was appointed in 1990 was Chairman of a Committee on Defence Expenditure by the then Prime Minister V.P. Singh, to analyse and advice on issues of India's Nuclear Doctrine and No First Use Policy. (The former COAS, General K Sundarji and Shri K Subrahmanyam were its members).

The Report of the CDE is not available in the public domain and could not be referred to for purposes of this book. Its principal recommendations relating to Higher Defence Management, as constructed from various discussions, media reports and articles are the creation of a Joint Chiefs of Staff as an adviser to the Defence Minister on all military issues. The CDE did not apparently recommend the appointment of a CDS but that the Joint Chiefs of Staff be headed by an Army Commander rank officer. Also, the creation of the JCS was not to compromise or diminish the access of the rights of the three Service Chiefs to the Defence Minister to present their respective views.

The CDE also apparently recommended the integration of the Ministry of Defence with the Services Headquarters with the Defence Secretary being nominated as the Principal Administrative Adviser to the Defence Minister. His functions would include coordination Perspective Plans, Budgets, Overall policies for administration, accounting, parliamentary matters, interface with other Ministries and Departments of the Government and matters relating to various States. The Ministry of Defence was recommended to be reorganised to play this revised role. 'Services Boards' were recommended to be set up for the management of individual Services to improve efficiency in all functional and administrative matters. Respective Chiefs of Staff were recommended to be made responsible for all revenue expenditure in respect of their Services to allow them flexibility and speedy decision making.

There were other recommendations the CDE is said to have made such as the closing down of some Ordnance Factories and low-technology Defence production units and harness the capacities in the private sector to obtain the goods they were producing; the integration of civil and military finance officers across the Ministry of Defence; enhance the participation of scientists, private industry, etc.

THE KARGIL REVIEW COMMITTEE (KRC) 1999

The Kargil Review Committee was set up in 1999 in the aftermath of the Kargil operations under the Chairmanship of Shri K Subrahmanyam, a doyen of Strategic Studies in India. It had as its members Lieutenant General KK Hazari, a former Vice Chief of army staff, and BG Verghese, a distinguished columnist and Shri Satish Chandra, the then Chairman of the Joint Intelligence Committee (JIC) was appointed its Member-Secretary.

The unique feature of this Committee was that it was not constituted under the Commissions of Inquiry Act and hence did not have formal authority to investigate, summon witnesses or requisition documents. However, it was provided 'the widest possible access to all relevant documents, including those with the highest classification' once it was clarified that the Committee had no mandate or intention to fix any responsibility on particular individuals or institutions. The following extract from the Committee's Report succinctly summarises the entire Civil–Military disconnect and its consequences on national security.

> *India is perhaps the only democracy where the Armed Forces are outside the apex government structure. The Chiefs of Staff have assumed the role of operational commanders of their respective forces rather than that of Chiefs of Staff to the Prime Minister and the Defence Minister. They simultaneously discharge the roles of operational commanders and national security planners/managers, especially in relation to future equipment and force postures. Most of their time is, however, devoted to their operational role, as is bound to happen. This has led to a number of negative results. Future–oriented long term planning suffers. Army Headquarters has developed a command rather than a staff culture. Higher decisions on equipment, force levels, and strategy are not collegiate but command oriented. The Prime Minister and Defence Minister do not have the benefit of the views and expertise of the Army Commanders and their equivalents in the navy and the Air Force so that higher level defence management decisions are more consensual and broad based. The present obsolete system has perpetuated the continuation of the culture of the British imperial theatre system of an India Command whereas what is required is a national Defence Headquarters. Most opposition to change comes from inadequate knowledge of the national security decision-making process elsewhere in the world and a reluctance to change the status quo and move away from considerations of parochial interest. The status quo is often mistakenly defended as embodying civilian ascendancy over the military, which is not the real issue. In fact, locating the Services Headquarters within the Government will further enhance civilian supremacy.*[5]

Major findings and observations of the Kargil Review Committee, relevant here are as follows:

(a) Several Indian Chiefs of Army Staff and Directors General Military Operations told the Committee that bringing to bear India's assumed conventional superiority was not a serious option in the last ten years for a variety of reasons; commitments in Sri Lanka, subsequent deployments in North east and Kashmir, and a drastic reduction in defence outlay.

(b) There was inadequate coordination at the ground level among Army intelligence and other agencies. This was lacking even at the Joint Intelligence Committee (JIC) because of low representation by DGMI at the assessment process and the DGMI representative not coming fully briefed on the latest situation.

(c) Though the new light rifle (5.56 mm INSAS) has been inducted into service, most troops are yet to be equipped with light rifles. Adequate attention has not been paid to lightening the load on infantry soldiers deployed in high altitudes. In broader terms, increasing the firepower and combat efficiency of infantrymen has also suffered as has the modernisation process as a whole. This needs to be speedily rectified.

(d) The Air Chief maintained that if air power was used, the country should be prepared for a Pakistani response. Therefore the relevant Air Commands and Units were activated. The CCS finally authorised the use of the Air Force on May 25,

(e) It is not widely appreciated that the primary responsibility for collecting external intelligence, including that relating to a potential adversary's military deployment, is vested in R&AW... Therefore it is R&AW which must provide intelligence about a likely attack...intelligence collection, coordination and follow-up were weak.

(f) The Intelligence Bureau (IB) is meant to collect intelligence within the country and is a premier agency for counter-intelligence. An issue that emerged which illustrated the systemic deficiencies existing at the time is that the IB did get certain inputs on activities in the FCNA region which were considered important enough by Director IB to be communicated to the Prime Minister, Cabinet Secretary,

Home Secretary and Director General Military Operations but not addressed to Secretary (R&AW), Chairman JIC, and the Director General Military Intelligence.

(g) The critical failure in intelligence was related to the absence of any information on the induction and de-induction of battalions and the lack of accurate data on the identity of battalions in the area opposite Kargil during 1998, the responsibility for obtaining which rested on the R&AW and, to a much less extent, on the DGMI.

(h) The Army makes six-monthly indents, and wherever necessary, special indents (regarding Intelligence) on R&AW. These indents and their prioritisation depend on the nature of the threat perception which, in turn, is shaped by inputs from the R&AW. This circular process entails the Army having to depend upon inputs from R&AW for its own threat assessment. In other words, the Indian threat assessment is largely a single track process dominated by R&AW.

(i) There are no checks and balances in the Indian intelligence system to ensure that the consumer gets all the intelligence that is available and is his due. There is no system of periodic and comprehensive intelligence briefings to the political class and to the Committee of Secretaries.

(j) In spite of continuing counter-intelligence operations over the past many years, there has been no integrated equipment policy in respect of the Army, Para-Military and Central Police Forces.

(k) The Kargil battle was fought with less than optimum communications capability. *While self-reliance and indigenisation are sound principles, the availability of critical equipment in time of combat is the supreme consideration that must govern equipment policy.*

(l) The DRDO is responsible for indigenising and constantly upgrading the country's weapons and equipment inventory and related supplies. The dilemma has always been to determine the correct balance between 'make' and 'buy'. There had been a number of instances were brought to the notice of the Committee in respect of which there have been significant cost and time overruns in the development and induction of indigenous weapons and equipment for the three Armed Services... *The fact is that the Services had to do without such items whereas Pakistan had not been similarly handicapped.*

A few pertinent recommendations made by the Kargil Review Committee are as follows:

(a) Members of the National Security Council, the senior bureaucracy servicing it and the Service Chiefs need to be continually sensitised to assessed intelligence pertaining to national, regional and international issues. This can be done through periodic intelligence briefings to the CCS with all supporting staff in attendance.

(b) The Army must be young and fit at all times. Therefore, instead of the present practice of having 17 years of colour service (as has been the policy since 1976), it would be advisable to reduce the colour service to a period of seven to ten years and, thereafter, release these officers and men for service in the country's paramilitary formations

(c) The Prime Minister and the Defence Minister do not have the benefit of views and expertise of the Army Commanders and their equivalents in the Navy and Air Force so that higher level defence management decisions are more consensual and broad based.... Locating Services headquarters in the government would in fact further enhance civilian supremacy, not dilute it.

(d) Structural reforms could bring about much closer and more constructive interaction between the Civil government and the Services, *The Committee is of the view that the present obsolete system, bequeathed to India by Lord Ismay, merits re-examination.* An effective and appropriate national security planning and decision making structure in India for the nuclear age is overdue, taking account of the revolution in Military Affairs and threats of proxy war and terrorism and the imperative of modernising the Armed forces.... *The Committee therefore recommends that the entire gamut of national security management and apex decision making and the structure and interface between the Ministry of Defence and the Armed Forces headquarters be comprehensively studied and re-organised.*

(e) One problem the DRDO faces is that the Armed Forces borrow unique features from weapons and equipment on offer from advanced military suppliers around the world and marry these in their General staff requirements. To make impossible demands... a partnership must be established between the Services and the DRDO to ensure the latter gets full backing and funding from the

Services and the former, in turn, get the indented equipment they require without undue delay.

A very strong caution is contained in the Epilogue to the Report, which reads:

> *There is both comfort and danger in clinging to any long established status quo. There will be many who suggest the most careful deliberation on the report. Procrastination has cost the nation dear. Others will no doubt advocate monumental change. Half measures will not do; synergy will be lost. The Committee, after very wide interaction, sign-posted directions along the path to peace ensuring progress, development and stability of the nation. How exactly the country should proceed to refashion its security-intelligence-development shield to meet the challenge of the 21st Century is for the Government, Parliament and Public opinion to determine. There is no turning away from that responsibility.*[6]

THE GROUP OF MINISTERS REPORT 2000

Subsequent to the presentation of the Kargil Committee Report before Parliament, the then Prime Minister, constituted a Group of Ministers on 17 April 2000 to review the national security system in its entirety and to implement the recommendations made by the Kargil Review Committee. To this end, four Task Forces were set up to examine different aspects of national security, namely (a) Internal security, (b) Intelligence, (c) Border Management and (d) Management of Defence.

The Task Force on Defence, the one relevant for this Study, was headed by Shri Arun Singh, the former Minister of State for Defence who had also headed the earlier Committee on Defence Expenditure (CDE). This Task Force agreed with the Kargil Review Committee on the need for restructuring of the Defence apparatus, but differed on how this needs to be achieved. Between the "evolutionary and incremental or revolutionary options" they chose to adopt the incremental one, it differed on how this should be done.

At the centre of the Reforms was the need to create the appointment of the Chief of Defence Staff (CDS) as also the Integrated Defence Staff (IDS), creation of a tri-services command at Andaman and Nicobar Command (ANC) and the Strategic Forces Command (SFC). The other aspect was the integration of the Services Headquarters with the Ministry of Defence.

As the three Service Headquarters have traditionally functioned as 'Attached Offices' of the Ministry of Defence, the procedure for consideration of proposals forwarded by them entailed files after being initiated and processed at the Service Headquarters, underwent the same process at the Ministry. This created problems as the military resented their logic being challenged by relatively junior ranking staff at the MoD.

There was also a 'parallel file system' in the Ministry of Defence which increased this resentment as it led to the Military coming to believe that they were 'not under political control but were under bureaucratic control'. Ironically, as mentioned before, the proposal made in the mid-sixties to integrate the Ministry of Defence with the Service Headquarters was not accepted by the Services on the logic that 'the military should stay away from the civilians'.

Arun Singh's own belief was that 'there are two broad components to this [civil-military] relationship – those involving the strategic and tactical issues concerning military operations where the advice must come predominantly from the military with the civil service component of MoD providing a historical background and an inter-ministerial view and matters involving issues like acquisitions, personnel, budgeting, and a host of similar issues where the civil MoD inputs can be vital for the political leadership in assessing military advice'.[7] He acknowledged the problems 'stemming from the lack of specialisation within MoD bureaucrats' and hence, ideally, he wanted to create a 'dedicated civilian national security civil service staff pool from which the Ministries of Defence/Home and other National Security entities can be drawn'. (A similar suggestion had also been made by the other task Force on Internal Security headed by Shri NN Vohra).

The Epilogue to the Group of Ministers' Report of 2000 states:

> *It is for the first time, in independent India's history, that a comprehensive review of the national security system in its entirety has been undertaken. This is most timely, as our security environment has inevitably experienced major changes in the preceding five decades. The apparatus and systems*

that we had inherited from the British are no longer suitable in this day and age. The biggest challenge, facing the country today, is the need to step up the pace of economic growth and to ensure the fair and equitable distribution of the fruits of such growth. However, rapid development coupled with distributive justice cannot be achieved, without first ensuring stable peace and security in the country. Hence, the task of effectively safeguarding the country's security assumes an overriding primacy and demands that the systemic reforms required for achieving this goal must be implemented without delay.[8]

MAJOR RECOMMENDATIONS OF THE GOM REPORT

Integration of Service Headquarters Into Government

In the organisational setup of the Government, as it exists now, besides Ministries and departments, there are either 'Attached Offices' or 'Subordinate Offices' which create an erroneous perception that the Armed Forces Headquarters do not participate in policy formulation and are outside the apex Governmental structure. In order to remove this impression, *the Service Headquarters may be designated as 'Integrated Headquarters' of the MoD for which the Transaction of Business Rules and Standing Orders should be appropriately amended.*

Though the Service Headquarters have always been associated in the decision-making process, the existing procedures involve multiplicity of levels/channels, which often lead to delays in decision-making. Given the size of the country and its substantial budget, the Report recommended to progressively decentralise decision making and delegate powers to the Service Headquarters, wherever feasible so as to ensure greater speed, higher levels of efficiency and accountability.

With a view to strike the right balance between the exercise of delegated administrative and financial authority and accountability, the Report proposed that the matter be examined in its totality by two committees headed respectively by Defence Secretary, on delegation of administrative powers, and the Financial Adviser (Defence Services) FA (DS) on the delegation of financial powers.

The Report also proposed that the (then) existing limits be revised to Rs. 50 crores and Rs. 100 crores for the Defence Minister and the Finance Minister, respectively.

CHIEF OF DEFENCE STAFF (CDS)

The COSC has not been effective in fulfilling its mandate. It needs to be strengthened by the addition of a CDS and a Vice-Chief of Defence Staff (VCDS). The CDS is required to be established for the following reasons:

(a) ***To Provide Single-Point Military Advice to the Government.*** Under the existing system, each of the Service Chiefs renders military advice to the civil political executive independent of one another, which the GOM Report considered to be unsatisfactory. Creation of a CDS would ensure provision of single point military advice to the civil political executive. *Before presenting his advice, the CDS will consult the Service Chiefs and will inform Government of the range of military advice and opinion with respect to the subject in hand. Individual Service Chiefs will have the right to present their own view where that is at variance with the CDS' views.*

(b) ***To Administer the Strategic Forces.*** As India is now a state with nuclear weapons, the highest importance must be attached to the creation of appropriate structures for the management and control of our nuclear weapons and strategic forces. The CDS should exercise administrative control, as distinct from operational military control over these strategic forces.

(c) ***To Enhance the Efficiency and Effectiveness of the Planning Process through Intra and Inter-Service Prioritisation.*** Under the existing system, each Service tends to advance its own capability without regard for inter-Service and even intra-Service prioritisation. *Accordingly, one of the most vital tasks that the CDS would be expected to perform is to facilitate efficiency and effectiveness in the planning/budgeting process to ensure the optimal and efficient use of available resources.* This could be carried out through intra-Service and inter-Service prioritisation of acquisitions and projects.

(d) ***To Ensure Required "Jointness" in the Armed Forces.*** The capabilities of the Armed Forces can be enhanced significantly, if rather than operating as three individual units, they operate with a high degree of "jointness" and in close tandem with one another in the conduct of various tasks, including training. Modern warfare demands a much higher degree of coordination in operations by all the three Services than ever before. Creation of a CDS would promote greater 'jointness' in the Armed Forces.

The CDS may be a 4-star officer drawn from one of the three Services in Rotation. He shall function as a permanent Chairman of the COSC with the VCDS as its Member-Secretary. Accordingly, he should rank primus inter pares in the COSC and function as the 'Principal Military Adviser' to the Defence Minister.

In order to support the CDS in the optimal exploitation of his role and functions, a Vice Chief of Defence Staff (VCDS) be appointed who would be responsible for the Defence Staff and report to the CDS.

Given India's nuclear status, there is a pressing need to establish a Strategic Forces Command, to manage all strategic forces.

In view of the growing strategic importance of the Andaman and Nicobar Group of islands, the replacement of the Fortress Commander Andaman and Nicobar (FORTAN) by a Joint Andaman and Nicobar Command has now become necessary.

The Role and Responsibilities of Defence Secretary

It is extremely important that there is no dilution in the role of the Defence Secretary as the 'Principal Defence Adviser' to the Defence Minister. Accordingly, it is felt that:

(a) The Defence Secretary should be officially designated in standing orders as the 'Principal Defence Adviser' and rank *primus inter pares* among the secretaries in the MoD. This measure is intended to reinforce the view that this individual, irrespective of pay scale or inter-service status, is a vital element in the higher management of Defence and should be so recognised unequivocally in civilian and military hierarchies.

(b) Standing orders need to be promulgated specifying that the Defence Secretary has the primary responsibility for advising the Defence

Minister on all policy matters and for the management of the Department, including financial management. As the Chief Accounting Officer for the Ministry, he is accountable to the Parliament for the expenditure of public money as budgeted by Parliament.

(c) The Defence Secretary should be responsible to the Defence Minister for the following:

   (i) Policy Advice.
   (ii) Supervising the Department of Defence.
   (iii) Co-ordinating the functioning of all departments in the Ministry.
   (iv) Co-ordinating the finalisation of the complete MoD Long Term Defence Perspective Plan (LTDPP), 5 year Plan, and the annual budget for approval by the Defence Minister.
   (v) Advising the Defence Minister on all matters relating to Parliament, Central Government and State Governments, in addition to advice generated by individual departments, and
   (vi) Co-ordinating all matters relating to personnel policies, terms and conditions of service, foreign postings and the like, with cadre Controlling Authorities in the MoD and with the Department of Personnel and Training (DoP&T) when required.

In a significant recommendation which has implications of the status of the Service Chiefs vis-à-vis the Defence Secretary, the Group of Ministers' Report proposed that 'The Defence Secretary will function as "Principal Defence Adviser" to the Defence Minister in a manner similar to the role to be performed by the CDS as the "Principal Military Adviser" and both will enjoy an equivalent status in terms of their working relationship as distinct from the Warrant of Precedence. Similarly, the Defence Secretary must enjoy an equivalent status vis-à-vis the Chiefs of Staff, in so far as their functional relationship is concerned. Meetings convened by the Defence Secretary on issues concerning him shall be attended by the CDS as necessary and vice versa. The Chiefs of Staff will also attend the meetings convened by the Defence Secretary, if required and vice versa.[9] The purpose of this arrangement is to ensure that the aspect of Warrant of Precedence does not vitiate the working environment of the Ministry.

Restructuring of the Ministry of Defence

The GOM Report recommended that In view of '... *dynamic and rapidly changing security environment, the Ministry of Defence (MoD) needs to be suitably restructured and strengthened. Far reaching changes in the structures, processes, and procedures in Defence Management would be required to make the system more efficient, resilient, and responsive. This would also ensure the maximisation of our defence capabilities through the optimal utilisation of our resources, potential, and establishment of synergy among the Armed Forces*'.

Enhancement of "Jointness" in the Armed Forces

The appointment of the CDS/VCDS with the designated defence staff and the cross-posting of officers in the Operations, Intelligence and Plans Directorates in the Service Headquarters would be the first major step in establishing synergy and 'Jointness' among the Armed Forces. This would be further fostered by strengthening the existing system of selections for higher appointments in the three Services and by making this process more objective. The COSC, chaired by the CDS, may function as the Review Board for all promotions to the rank of Commander-in-Chief (C-in-C) and equivalent. The recommendations of the COSC for such promotions should be forwarded to the Defence Secretary for obtaining the Defence Minister's approval. Where such recommendations are at variance with the Annual Confidential Report (ACR) matrices, the COSC must record reasons that weighed with it in making its recommendations. This procedure is expected to introduce the much needed transparency in the system of higher appointments.

Promotion Boards: Furthermore, with a view to ensure the utmost objectivity in the selection process, the Defence Minister's queries on Promotion Boards for different levels may be analysed by the Defence Secretary and the CDS who may, thereafter, make joint recommendations to the Defence Minister in this regard.

Restructuring of MoD and Service Headquarters

Consequent upon the creation of the CDS/VCDS/Defence Staff and the Procurement Board related structures, the GROUP OF MINISTERS Report stated that *"the organisational structure of the Department of Defence, Service Headquarters and Inter-Service Organisations (ISO)" will need to be reviewed. The Committee headed by the Defence Secretary, recommended earlier in the Report to look into the delegation of administrative powers should also finalise the details of such restructuring. The Report simultaneously stressed that the Services Headquarters would also require 'proper restructuring to take account of the changes being introduced'.*[10]

Planning and Budgeting Defence Planning

Charting their vision for the future planning mechanism and procedures, the Report stated that so far, individual Services have prepared their long term perspective plans. However, with the induction of the CDS (which the Report recommended) and other related structures, there would be a need to prepare "a holistic and integrated defence perspective plan for 15-20 years through a rigorous process of Inter-Service and Intra-Service prioritisation". It further added that '*the Five Year Defence Plans by the Services should be prepared on the basis of the LTDPP*' and that these be followed up by analysis and preparations of the Joint Services Plan by the VCDS, which may be finalised through consultation between the CDS and the Defence Secretary.

Further, '*The defence planning process incorporating the Long Term Defence plan, Five Year plan and Annual Budget should be revised at the earliest*' and '*The MoD and the CDS may be directed to ensure timely completion of the LTDPP and five yearly/annual defence plans, apart from introducing all suggested measures to bring about efficiency in defence expenditure*'. It also added *that 'the Ministry of Finance, while deciding on annual budgets must keep in view the requirements of defence plans*'.

To ensure the effectiveness of the planning exercise, the Defence Minister's directive should be issued at least 12 months before the commencement of the next Five Year Plan. This will form the conceptual basis for the Defence Plan. The Ministry of Finance should give a firm indication of the availability of financial resources, for a period of five years, at least 6 months before the commencement of the ensuing Five Year Plan.

To obtain the maximum value for money, the formulation of Services Equipment Policy Statements (SEPS) is required to be co-ordinated with the Perspective Planning and Services futuristic requirements.

Defence Budgeting: The Report highlights that optimal utilisation of resources cannot be achieved unless greater emphasis and attention is given to the process of budget formulation and implementation, including forecasting, monitoring and control. In this context, it felt that *"capital schemes in Service Headquarters' budgets should be included only if reasonable assurances of contract conclusion and some payment within the financial year exist".*[11]

Similarly, only those capital schemes should be included in the Service Headquarters' Priority Procurement Plan and annual budget, where there is adequate evidence that technical and commercial evaluation, leading to contracting and initial payment, can be completed in the relevant financial year. There is also a need for rigorous prioritisation and the order of charge on the budget being established with reference to the plan objectives.

Manpower and Staffing Issues: In view of the fact that the number of manpower classifications in the Armed Forces is excessive, the GOM Report recommended a review and simplifications of classifications in a time-bound manner. It recommended Committees be set up under the Chairmanship of Additional Secretary in the Department of Defence to *'examine and identify measures for increasing cost effectiveness in the employing organisations in the Department of Defence'* besides *'better utilisation of Armed Forces Headquarters (AFHQ) Civil Service officers within the Ministry of Defence'.*

Civil–Military Interface: The establishment of a civil–military liaison mechanism at various levels from Command Headquarters to operative formations at the ground level is essential to smoothen the relationship during times of stress and to prevent friction and alienation of the local population. In this respect, the Group of Ministers *inter alia* recommended the following:

(a) The Unified Headquarters in the States of the North East and Jammu and Kashmir (J&K) which are geared primarily to deal with insurgency situations in the relevant States, be further streamlined.

(b) At the State level, a Core Group of existing Civil–Military liaison forum may be set up to identify the problem areas and evolve a system of smooth mobilisation and thereafter, to meet the logistic needs of the Army. At the district level also, a group may be set up from the mobilisation stage onwards comprising representatives of the district administration and the Army, if available. It clarified that while this 'civil-military liaison mechanism may not be essential for all States, but can be institutionalised in the States of Gujarat, Rajasthan, Punjab, J&K, Haryana, Delhi, Uttar Pradesh, Sikkim, West Bengal, Assam and Arunachal Pradesh'.

(c) Although in some states formal Civil–Military Liaison structures already exist, problems of lack of communication, co-ordination and even misunderstandings between the civilian and the military officials persist and certain measures were suggested to build mutual trust. These included reviving the earlier tradition of military and civil officials posted in the field making social calls on the occasion of their joining the station for 'a conscious effort must be made by the Services and MoD to promote active social interaction between the civilians and the Armed Forces'.

There is also somewhat unusual recommendations for civilian(s) in the MoD being *"provided certain facilities available to the Armed Forces, like membership of clubs, medical facilities etc., so that they develop a sense of belonging to the Defence establishments and vice versa" and for setting up of a "composite group of representatives of the Ministries of Home, Defence, and the Defence Forces may be set up to undertake an in-depth examination of the civil-military interaction problems and bring out a manual on civil-military interface, incorporating practical measures for Implementation, not only at the formal but also at the informal level".*

Naresh Chandra Task Force

A significant segment of Services Officers community viewed the very institution of the Naresh Chandra Task Force (under the Chairmanship of Shri Naresh Chandra, a distinguished Bureaucrat who had been the Defence, Home and Cabinet Secretaries as also our Ambassador to the USA), to be a means of scuttling the Group of Ministers' recommendations and bringing to the table a watered-down set of proposals that would assuage the Services concerns to some extent without diluting the essential civilian controlled command apparatus.

Unfortunately for those with such intent, the Task Force did not oblige, nor did it reiterate the far-reaching recommendations of the Group of Ministers' Report in full measure. The Report itself is not in the public space, but appears to have stopped half-way house, as gleaned from the various recommendations it has reportedly made from a perusal of articles in open literature:

(a) The Services HQ being given a specific role under the AOB and TOB Rules 1961, with the responsibility for the defence of the country being placed on the Services rather than on the Defence Secretary as at present. The Services Headquarters are to be designated as 'Departments' of the Government of India under the Ministry of Defence, with the internal administration of each department being under the respective Vice Chiefs.

(b) Induction of Military personnel into the Ministry of Defence, which would bring in professional knowledge and advice seemingly lacking at present. Their participation in the decision-making chain would also enable considered decisions on prioritisation, etc., which would rationalise budget utilisation.

(c) Appointment of a Permanent Chairman, Chiefs of Staff Committee who would coordinate and prioritise long-term procurement plans, administer tri-services institutions and agencies, the A&N Command as also other Commands such as the Special Forces Command. The PC COSC would also provide single-point military advice to the Government with direct access to the Raksha Mantri. The PC COSC is intended to be a precursor to the eventual appointment of the CDS on which a decision could be taken in due course. His appointment would set in motion the development of appropriate structures to effect tri-services integration.

(d) The Service Chiefs also to have direct to the Raksha Mantri on individual service aspects.

(e) The Department of Defence to administer all aspects with tri-services implications as also residual aspects, including the coordination between various departments of the Ministry of Defence, Defence Budget, control of Defence lands and properties, CSD, etc.

Follow-up on the NCTF Recommendations

The NCTF recommendations were discussed at a meeting of the National Security Council under the Chairmanship of the Prime Minister in April 2013. The Strategic Policy Group (SPG) headed by the National Security Adviser was therefore tasked to examine those recommendations which included those pertaining to the working relations between the Ministry of Defence and the Services Headquarters, the appointment of a Permanent Chairman COSC, cross-posting of officers between the Ministry of Defence and the Services Headquarters.

On its part, the Ministry of Defence also reviewed the NCTF's recommendations. On the creation of the appointment of Permanent Chairman, COSC, though this was a somewhat diluted version of the CDS recommended by the Group of Ministers in 2001, it stuck to its earlier view not to accept a change in the status quo. One of the reasons for this stance of the Ministry of Defence are that the proposal to appoint a CDS did not find unanimous acceptance even within the three Services. The 'smaller Services' felt their own interests would not be given due importance and they may be overwhelmed.

There was no divergence in the views of the three Services Headquarters on the other proposal for cross-posting of officers to and from the Ministry of Defence, the merits of which are obvious. The beneficiary in fact would be the Ministry of Defence itself which would have seen an induction of much lacking technical expertise not available within its overwhelmingly generalist Staff. This single move would also have given some substance to the 'integration' process which so far is considered only 'cosmetic'. Even such a self-beneficial proposal has not been recommended by the Ministry of Defence on the plea that the present system was working well.

Certain apprehensions have been expressed confidentially by senior Defence Ministry officials. These are firstly that such a move would not be in the overall interests of either national security nor of the Services, as Defence Forces officers are at no stage formally trained to execute governmental responsibilities. Their command structure would not allow for rational 'considered' decision making with each functionary in the hierarchy expressing his own views on file. This would degenerate into a top-driven authoritarian decision mechanism. On the other hand, the 'Command' structure of the Forces is a 'desirable inherent trait' to efficiently execute their executive responsibilities, particularly in the realm of military operations.

Second, it de facto brings the Services into the 'Central Staffing Scheme' and furthers aspirations for prospective entry into other Departments and Ministries of the Government. From a Civilian perspective, this, in principle would be undesirable.

Another interesting mention by one middle level functionary is that such a move would 'provide the Services with a peek into assessments of their own internal functioning' and those who adopt candid honest postures' are bound to face retribution once they return to their respective Services'. (If one understands the present culture of the Services, this concern is not devoid of some merit).

The former Defence and External Affairs Minister, Shri Jaswant Singh, in his book *Defending India* has summed up the insolence of the Ministry of Defence and thereby of the Government of India to hold back the reform process as follows:

> *The Defence Ministry, in effect becomes the principal destroyer of the cutting edge of the military's morale, ironic considering that the very reverse of it is their responsibility. The sword arm of the State gets blunted by the State itself.*[12]

The below-mentioned extract from Curzon's pleadings to the Secretary of State, in which Curzon himself quotes Lord Dufferin (attention to which was drawn by a very Senior Bureaucrat) would enable this discussion to conclude on a note of balance:

> *...I have known military proposals put forward at Army Headquarters which were inconsistent with the fundamental principles of the policy of the Government, or with the facts of the situation. A department which is charged with the custody of the records and traditions of Government can issue warning against any such errors.*[13]

This debate remains ongoing.

NOTES

1. General Rao, Krishna K.V., *In the Service of the Nation – Reminiscences* (Penguin Books India Ltd, 2001), p. 143.
2. Rao, op. cit., p. 155.
3. Rao, op. cit., p. 157.
4. Ibid.
5. Kargil Review Committee Report. (Note: the Union Government vide its order dated July 29, 1999 constituted a Committee to look into the episode with the following Terms of Reference:-
   i. To review the events leading up to the Pakistani aggression in the Kargil district of Ladakh in Jammu and Kashmir; and
   ii. To recommend such measures as are considered necessary to safeguard national security against such armed intrusions.

   The Committee comprised four members namely K Subrahmanyam (Chairman), Lieutenant General (Retd) K K Hazari, B G Verghese and Satish Chandra, Secretary, National Security Council Secretariat who was also designated as Member-Secretary.
6. Kargil Review Committee Report.
7. Mukherjee, Anit, 'Failing to Deliver : Post-Crises Defence Reforms in India, 1998-2010', IDSA Occasional Paper No 18 (March 2011).
8. Group of Ministers Report on 'Reforming the National Security System' (Ministry of Defence).
9. Ibid.
10. Ibid.
11. Ibid.
12. Singh, Jaswant, *Defending India*, Palgrave Macmillan, 1998.
13. Khera, S.S. *India's Defence Problem*, Orient Longman, 1977, p. 8.

CHAPTER 8

HIGHER DEFENCE MANAGEMENT

BAGGAGE OF HISTORY

The 'initial liability' in regard to the Armed Forces borne by decision makers at the time of Independence has been explained by Shri K Subrahmaniam as follows:

> *In order to develop an understanding of our defence policy in post-Independence India, it is essential to look at the roots of that policy during the freedom struggle.... Since Gandhi was a firm advocate of non-violence, Indian defence preparedness was not given the attention it deserved.... There is also the view that Jawaharlal Nehru was anti-militarist in his orientation and as an advocate of peace and non-alignment, neglected the role of military power in International relations. During the early years of the first cold war, what India was advocating at that stage could easily have been justified in real-politic terms and strategic rationality. However, given the Indian environment and the traditions of the Indian freedom struggle, the argument advanced by Indians was couched in moralistic and ethical terms. The dividing line between strategic rationality and international morality is very thin indeed.*[1]

THE NEHRUVIAN LEGACY

In this backdrop, the Nehruvian ethic became binding on policy makers. The scope for 'strategic manoeuvre' became limited when, in June 1961, India accepted the following clauses post the Bandung Conference:

- A country shall not align or favour with Any Military Block (NATO or Warsaw) and should follow an independent policy based on the principle of peaceful co-existence.
- It should neither be a member of multilateral military alliances concluded in the context of great power conflict nor should it aspire to join them.
- An agreement on regional defence pact can be concluded without prejudice to join any of the military block or order to safeguard its sovereignty.
- A member country can lease military base(s) to a foreign power with sole motive to preserve self-independence without joining military blocks.

This agreement was signed around the very time when the then Army Chief, Gen KS Thimayya had brought to the knowledge of the Defence Minister and under controversial circumstances, of the Prime Minister, limitations in Indian force strengths and capabilities to meet the rising prospect of a Chinese attack. It is the perception in the military that they had not been consulted or involved while considering the draft terms that constrained a nation in seeking external assistance when confronted by a stronger adversary. The issue for debate is whether real politic had been sacrificed at the alter of assumption of a vacuous principled stance of 'high morals'.

VARYING PERCEPTIONS

General VP Malik, the former Chief of Army Staff and Chairman COSC during the Kargil Operations, has in his book *India's Military Conflicts and Diplomacy* discussed extensively the nature of the Politico-Military interface in India. His assessment is that '*over the years, instead of maintaining political control over the military, as exists in all democracies, India managed to develop a unique system of bureaucratic control over the military through civilian bureaucrats in the Ministry of Defence*'. [2] He goes on to add that '*Even today, there is little discourse between political and military leaders on the dynamics of defence planning and military capabilities for conflict contingencies. The Chiefs of the three Services are seldom invited to the Cabinet Committee on Security (CCS) to discuss the security environment dynamics except in an emergency, and never on issues concerning defence planning. Strategic Planning thus remains a grey area.*'[3]

To stress his argument, Gen Malik quotes Defence Analyst Kanti Bajpai's observation that '*while we worry that the military might stray across into the civilian sphere, there is growing sense that the balance is being damaged by the civilians. Civilian authorities have made mistakes – some of omission but others of commission. Civilians have not sufficiently involved the military in issues where military advice and involvement is proper and vital, that is on issues relating to national security. The military's role in threat assessment and military acquisitions has been unduly restricted. Its thinking on nuclear weapons has never been sought or discussed*'.[4]

The former Air Chief, ACM PV Naik, while addressing a Seminar to mark the 10th anniversary of the Arun Singh Committee reignited the Chief of Defence Staff (CDS) controversy when he claimed 'that it was not needed' emphasising that there existed serious concerns within the Services themselves on the '*significant problems in tactical interoperability, defence planning and overall coordination*' due to which '*the defence reforms process, initiated over a decade ago, has largely failed to deliver*'.

As Anit Mukherjee, formerly a scholar at the IDSA has in his book *Defense Planning in India: Role of Civil–Military Relations* states candidly '*that the services lack the capability to operate seamlessly has been proven time and again in operations*'. Giving an example from the deployment of the Indian Peace Keeping Force in Sri Lanka, he states that '*the army used to embed its radio detachments with naval ships and air force attack helicopters to enable communication links. Among the few instances where the army requested naval gunfire support, the navy engaged targets two kilometres away! More recently, during the Kargil war in 1999, Air Force jets did not have the capability to communicate with troops operating on the front. In fact, the Air Force did not have secure, encrypted communication capability (and still does not) in some of its planes, forcing them to fly in radio silence – a characteristic of the WW II era.*'[5]

POLICY FORMULATION AND DECISION-MAKING STRUCTURES

The Constitution of India lays down that *'the Supreme Command of the Defence Forces of the Union shall be vested in the President of India and the exercise thereof shall be regulated by law'.* This, however, is ancillary to the position of the President as the Constitutional Head of State in a Parliamentary democracy wherein he acts on the advice of the Council of Ministers headed by the Prime Minister. The President obviously cannot be both, a Constitutional head on the civil side as also a Military Supremo. Article 83(2) of the Constitution stipulates that 'without prejudice to the generality' of Article 83(1), vests executive power in the President 'to be exercised with the law'. It also stipulates that the President's position as C-in-C 'shall be regulated by law'.

Major decisions relating to the security of the nation are taken by the Cabinet Committee on Security, chaired by the Prime Minister and include the Defence, Home, External Affairs and Finance Ministers besides such other Ministers who are nominated as members by the Prime Minister. While the very broad policies are discussed and approved by the CCS, it is the Ministry of Defence, headed by the Defence Minister, which maintains direct control and oversight over the Armed Forces, with all functional level policy and administrative decisions being taken at the Ministry of Defence.

This is the zone of functional control in which the scales of 'Civil–Military balance' oscillate and has therefore been the focal point for this text. Under extant rules, regulations, procedures and traditions there is no formal requirement for the Services Chiefs to be even 'in attendance' for the CCS Meetings. *Apart from this, the participation of the Armed Forces in policy formulation and decision making limits to a contributory role to forums under the Defence Minister and other levels in the Ministry of Defence.*

The Cabinet Committee on Security (CCS)

Cabinet Committee on Security is the highest political decision making authority for security-related matters. Chaired by the Prime Minister it has as members the Ministers for Home Affairs, Finance, External Affairs, besides the Defence Minister. Other Ministers and attendees, including the Services Chiefs attend on an 'as required' basis. The CCS considers all immediate, short and long-term defence actions and policies and is serviced by the Cabinet Secretariat.

The Defence Minister's Committee (DMC)

The DMC is chaired by the Raksha Mantri and comprises Ministers of State in the MoD, Service Chiefs, Defence Secretary, Secretary Defence Production, Scientific and Financial Advisors to Raksha Mantri. The Committee interprets National Aims and Objectives as determined by the CCS and formulates policies and evolves plans. Meetings of the DMC are not held as per a laid down or priorly announced schedule, which was so when initially constituted. The forum hence does not lend itself to be one where the Services HQ can plan to raise issues or place proposals before to obtain speedy decisions. One senior officer opined that the DMC Meetings are called for when the Ministry of Defence on their part have an agenda to fulfil, not the Services HQ.

Committees of the Ministry of Defence

(a) The Defence Acquisition Council (DAC) chaired by the Defence Minister considers all major procurement proposals for the Defence Services.

(b) The Defence Minister's (Production & Supply) Committee deals with matters relating to indigenous production of Defence Stores, equipment and import substitution. It also reviews from time to time the mobilisation plans for Defence Production.

(c) The Defence Minister's Appellate Committee on Pensions to consider appeals in respect of claims to disability and family pensions of the personnel of the Armed Forces.

(d) The Defence Research and Development Council is responsible for coordinating and indicating general direction of policy for scientific research relating to Defence and the development of or improvement in material required by the Armed Forces.

Subordinate Committees of the DMC

The Defence Minister's Committee has two Sub-Committees, viz. Principal Personnel Officers Committee and Principal Supply Officers Committee with the Ministry of Defence, Ministry of Defence (Finance) and Services Headquarters representation. These Sub-Committees are presided over by the senior most Services representative on the Sub-Committee on rotational basis. These Sub-Committees meet regularly at the direction of the Defence Minister's Committee or at the request of any member of the Sub-Committee.

Committee on Defence Planning (CDP)

Headed by the Cabinet Secretary and this includes Service Chiefs, Secretaries for Defence, Defence Production, Finance, Foreign and the Planning Commission. Besides integrating Defence matters into national development plans, the CDP is also mandated to review geo-strategic developments, review objectives of defence efforts, harmonise foreign policy, review defence priorities and to review defence plans drawn up by the Ministry of Defence.

Organisations outside the Ministry of Defence

While all Major strategic and security-elated decisions are taken by the Cabinet Committee on Security (CCS) policy formulations and directives are considered and approved by the National Security Council (NSC), established in 1998 under the Chairmanship of the Prime Minister. It comprises three tiers, namely:

(a) **The National Security Council (NSC):** Chaired by the Prime Minister with the Foreign, Home, Finance and Defence Ministers and the National Security Advisor as its members, the NSC undertakes long-term reviews and decides on long-term policy options, coordinates intelligence assessments to evolve comprehensive analysis and draw up the best policy options besides determining the size and structure of nuclear forces, the command control and communication systems and their final employment.

(b) **The Strategic Policy Group (SPG):** (Chaired by the Cabinet Secretary with the three Service Chiefs, Governor Reserve Bank of

India, Secretaries of key Ministries/Depts, Dir R&AW and Dir IB. The erstwhile Joint Intelligence Committee (JIC) was converted to being the Secretariat of the SPG to provide long-term intelligence information. It is the highest forum with a formal participation of the Services Chiefs.

(c) **The National Security Advisory Board (NSAB):** This board comprises eminent experts from various fields including external and internal security, Strategic Analysts experts on Defence Science and Technology, who are appointed by the Prime Minister. It provides long-term analysis and prognosis for the NSC.

Parliamentary Oversight

The Standing Committee on Defence and the Public Accounts Committee exercise notional oversight over the functioning of the Ministry of Defence.

VOIDS IN SECURITY ARCHITECTURE AND PLANNING PROCESS

It is the constant refrain of the Defence Services that the participation of the Military in the higher decision making, which they claim as their raison d'être and hence a rightful role, has been reduced to a peripheral position with bureaucrats, diplomats and even Police Officers dominating the security and intelligence control architecture. In their view, the indifference of the political class has been a major contributor which is in sharp contrast to the obtaining position in other nations where there is a well-developed synergy between the military and the political leadership. In contrast, India has the opposite happening, of the military being removed or distanced from a direct interface between decision makers and the decision making process. It is the Defence Ministry bureaucracy that has the last say in almost all major defence decisions but without any corresponding responsibility. In retrospect, the Defence Services feel strongly that the control structures recommended by Lord Ismay, though well intended, did not have requisite in-built checks and balances to prevent a determined bureaucracy to move itself into a position of near absolute control of the military.

CONTROL MECHANISMS OF THE MINISTRY OF DEFENCE

The Ministry of Defence is staffed by two broad categories of personnel – at the highest levels are officers largely belonging to the IAS. The Defence Secretary is invariably an IAS Officer as are the Additional and Joint Secretaries, though a few officers from other Central Services have intermittently been appointed as Joint Secretaries and on very few occasions, as Additional Secretary.

While a select set of appointments even at Director level at are also held by IAS Officers, most other Director, Deputy Secretary and subordinate appointments are manned by officials posted under the 'Central Staffing' from a plethora of cadres including interestingly, the Indian Postal Service. IAS officers have a normal Delhi tenure of five years in the course of which they could hold two or even three appointments. Hence the average tenure at the Defence Ministry is less than three years with there being no recent case of an IAS Officer having had a full tenure of five years in the Ministry of Defence.

It is the Defence Secretary alone, besides some other Secretary level appointments who, through an amendment to FR 56, has an assured tenure of two years from the date of appointment notwithstanding the date of his superannuation.

The Defence Services have consistently raised, obviously based on long experience in interacting with the Defence Ministry, that the management of national defence is a 'specialist' job and it is imperative that those with responsibility to manage affairs relating to the defence of the country need to possess some depth of understanding of issues in their operational and/or military context. Defence Services officers, except to very few technical appointments, are not posted to 'mainline' appointments in the Ministry of Defence nor do they form part of the pool of officers from various cadres eligible under the Central Staffing to be posted to Central Government Ministries and Departments. The Defence Services have long argued that posting their officers to the Ministry of Defence, if not other Ministries, would infuse 'professionalism' and 'expertise' into their staffing.

The argument against doing so is that it would place a Service Officer in a position of conflict with himself by requiring him to retain his independence of thought and objectivity against the grain of recommendations forwarded by his own Service Headquarters. As eventually, all proposals of consequence, howsoever technical, are required to be understood and approved by non-military officers and Ministers and it would serve the decision-making process better if the technicalities in a proposal are disambiguated and the implications of each strand elaborated in the proposals itself.

Oversight over Policy Implementation

The Allocation of Business Rules 1961 categorically mandate all policies to be formulated in the Secretariats of various Ministries and Departments. The Services Headquarters, which remain to be 'Attached Offices' of the Ministry of Defence, quite deliberately, were kept outside the realm of policy formulation. The Bureaucrat's line of argument is that Charter and duties of the Services HQ and the control structures are well defined and time tested. The issue is one of 'misplaced aspirations' on the part of Services personnel, who are professionals with a defined role and are required to function within laid down parameters.

Control of Military Operations

All Military Operations undertaken by the Military are done so with due prior approval of the Government of India. This approval carries with it an aspect of accountability as also of accounting. Expenditure of human resource or material in any form or manner which is incurred without prior sanction, say in self-defence, would require 'ex post facto' sanction. There is thus no discretion with the Armed Forces to *suo moto* conduct operations at their own initiative.

Budgetary Controls

All expenditures of the Armed Forces are met through allocations of funds for the Defence Ministry in the Union Budget as approved by Parliament. The Armed Forces look for appropriate allocations to meet the rising costs of running their Forces as also meeting planned and emergent procurements. However, given the need for a long term view of future requirements, the long lead times between approving a procurement and the required stores becoming available, high dependence on imports to meet our requirement of military hardware, the allocation for budget is drawn out over a long term plan which in turn is divided into shorter Five Year and Annual Plans. The current phase of defence modernisation, derives from the Armed Forces' long-term integrated perspective plan (LTIPP) 2012-27 covering the periods of the 12th, 13th and 14th Five Year Defence Plans.

There are, however, no fixed principles on the basis of which the allocations are made in the defence budget to ensure that adequate outlay is available to match planned procurements. It has been a long-standing plea of the Armed Forces that a determined percentage of the GDP be set aside for allocation to Defence which would provide requisite stability to planning. Budgetary allocations are, however, made to adequately meet the operating costs of the Services including pay and allowances, meet committed liabilities and meet costs of accepted and approved modernisation projects and schemes. Defence expenditure as a percentage of GDP is more an indicative statistic that serves its purpose of comparison with other nations. There is no policy or assurance for it to be a particular percentage of the GDP and unlikely to be.

Meanwhile Defence allocations have remained consistently short of that considered necessary to carry our credible future planning. *An opinion is often expressed that projecting demands which cannot be met is as pointless as allocating a budget that is not adequate to meet the modernisation needs. As is well known, persistent neglect of adequate and timely procurements has taken a toll not only on the crucial aspect of stock of ammunition as also on serviceability levels of the equipment, weapon systems and other platforms.*

As stated by Amit Cowshish, a former Additional Financial Advisor now a Distinguished Fellow at the IDSA, '*in the absence of a broad framework of a fully synchronised and accurately costed defence plan, financial management is limited to monitoring of expenditure against allotment with a view to ensuring full utilisation of the budget*'.[6]

There is an obvious clamour amongst the three Forces for a larger apportionment for their ends. Allocations being limited, there comes a need for prioritisation. Though approval of expenditures are retained by the Ministry of Defence there has been some delegation of powers to functionaries in the Services Headquarters. The exercise of Budget planning as such is coordinated by HQ IDS. Service Officers argue that allocations as a whole should be much higher and the course of defence modernisation should never be slowed down for lack of funds.

Control over Procurements

Defence Procurement is a domain entirely controlled by the Ministry of Defence with the Services' role being drawing up of requirements, requisite SQRs determining numbers and submission of their proposals. *It is a long-standing grievance on the part of the Services that the procurement process is slow and tortuous and in the ultimate, it is they who face the consequences of delays, and in their perception, incompetence and inefficiency on the part of decision-making, production and supply Agencies over who they have no control.*

This has been the position since Independence and hence the Ministry of Defence must accept responsibility for the obtaining state of affairs as have been collated from views of several interviewees are mainly:

(a) Defence PSUs and Ordnance Factories, with over one lakh industrial personnel, are inefficient without corporate work ethic with prohibitive production costs. The 'welfare' need to keep a production line ongoing assumes primacy over the 'professional' need to ensure efficiencies and loudest bang for the buck.

(b) Technological planning and development is a weak component and needs to be bridged through coordinated approach of R&D, production agencies and users. The 'loud' claims of the DRDO are tepidly viewed within the Services as hollow.

The Defence Procurement Procedure' first promulgated in 2002 has been 'updated' and reformulated' several times, most recently in April 2016. Most former Services interviewees expressed satisfaction with changes brought in by DPP-2016 but emphasised that Defence Services must have a stake and be completely involved in the identification of equipment to be procured and the selection of the right supplier. Many also agree that commercial aspects could be left for decision by the civil side.

Control of Promotions to and Appointments in Senior Ranks

Promotion of Officers to all Flag ranks (Brig/Commodore/Air Commodore) and above are approved by the Government of India. Whereas appointments as Chiefs of Staff, Army Commanders and Principal Staff Officers and certain other appointments such as Dir Gen Military Operations are made with the approval of the Appointments Committee of the cabinet (ACC), postings, and appointments of all other Lt Gens and Maj Gens and equivalent ranks are made with the approval of the Ministry of Defence.

While by and large this control is notional and recommendations for postings to various appointments in these ranks, recommended with the approval of the respective Service Chiefs, are generally accepted, the Ministry of Defence does maintain a close oversight and raises observations in regard to the suitability of a particular officer for the appointment recommended by the Services Headquarters. The factors the Ministry of Defence bears in mind while analysing proposals are qualifications, experience and professional competence to execute responsibilities, adherence to norms, policies, regulations prescribed particularly in cases where minimum residual service is involved, favouritism especially if rooted in regimental loyalties, past functional association with the same chain of officials, any apparent favouritism and whether as per their records and inputs available with them, there are reasons to apprehend an inability of the officer to execute his functions freely and objectively. *In fairness to the Ministry of Defence, it needs mention that all Services Officers interviewed and with who this aspect was raised accepted the existing system to be fair and objective and as being a necessity.*

One jarring case in recent history mentioned was one pertaining to the promotion to the rank of Lt Gen in the late 1990s of an officer who had otherwise superannuated from service, though on merits, that case differed from the similar past case of ACM PC Lal.

An interesting recent media report on the book written by K Arun on his late father Vice Admiral MEA Krishnan the 1971 War Naval Commander merits being quoted. According to Arun, Admiral Krishnan had been given an extension to serve up to 1975. However, it is that very year that Prime Minister Indira Gandhi had clamped the emergency during which period 'the privileges her son enjoyed are well known'. Arun mentions of Sanjay Gandhi having interviewed his father when he was running for the post of CNS in 1975. To quote '*Incredible as it may seem, one of the interviews was conducted by a young man, who held no elected office, Cabinet or in fact, any official government position, but wielded immense power by virtue of the fact that he was the Prime Minister's son – Sanjay Gandhi*'. The book adds that 'while reviewing Krishnan's file, Sanjay remarked: '*Admiral, you have an impeccable service record, but you have a reputation of being a very strong personality*'.[7]

Command and Control Aspects of 'Aid to Civil Authority'

Lt Gen Nanavatty in his book *Internal Armed Conflict in India* states that '*in internal armed conflict, civil military relations are rendered (very) complex. Dealing with conflict is a function of the Ministry of Home Affairs (MHA) at the level of the Union Government and the Department of Home Affairs in each State. The Officials of the Min of Def are not involved and prefer to remain that way*'.

Lt Gen Nanavatty further states that '*At the level of MHA, institutionalised interface with Army Headquarters is absent. This virtually denies Army Headquarters formal access to deliberations at the level of the Ministry...and contents itself by presenting its views if and when they are sought*" and that "*In the State, the senior Military Commander will find himself junior to in rank and status to the Chief Secretary and the Director General of Police*". He further adds that '*the responsibility for the resolution of internal Armed Conflict may well be that of the civil government but the role of the military leader is not circumscribed*'.

In Gen Nanavatty's assessment, *'Poor Centre-State and Civil–Military relations have discouraged the articulation of a comprehensive doctrine for the management and resolution of internal armed conflict in India. He stresses the imperative to formulate, articulate and adopt a joint civil military doctrine involving the three key arms of Government – the civil administration, police and Army, for the conduct of counter insurgency campaign. Equally important is the need for the political executive to understand, appreciate and approve of such a doctrine and the will to apply it in practice.'*[8]

THE FAULTLINES

To sum up, the major fault lines that emerge from discussions across the civil–military divide are:

(a) Lack of an institutional direct interface of the Military with the Political Authority.

(b) While Political control of the Military is well established, the Civil bureaucracy has emerged to occupy the central ground and marginalise the military leadership. The Ministry of Defence, responsible for the defence of the nation, is not adequately equipped with professionally trained functionaries. It needs restructuring and professional staffing.

(c) The Defence Minister functions through far too many Committees with varied members which slow down the decision making process and obfuscates authority. This results in there being lack of accountability commensurate with responsibility in the Ministry of Defence.

(d) There is an absence of an effective joint defence planning process. Present apparatus headed by CISC more 'nodal' with no authority to overrule. Needs empowerment.

(e) Budget allocation is not linked to requirements, which impacts comprehensive capability building.

(f) Procurement continues to be viewed as 'expenditure' and 'Accountant' driven rather than being driven by 'requirements of the present and future battle-zone'.

(g) Lack of credible military intelligence estimates in spite of revised arrangements.

(h) Capability and capacity deficit to deal with changing paradigms of threats and challenges on account of following:

(i) Inability of COSC to provide substantive cohesive and integrated advice on important military matters.

(ii) There being no Permanent Chairman for the COSC, a degree of *conflict of interest in his dual roles as Chairman COSC and Service Chief. The inter-service conflicts* carry forward to Higher Committees where Service Chiefs are members. *(This is the fault line that Service Officers mention has been exploited by the bureaucracy has exploited to keep the Services divided and proliferate their control over Services decision making and functioning).*

There is a lack of synchronisation among various Services at their own level, thereafter between the Services and the Ministry of Defence and other Security related organisations. As expressed by one interviewee, *the 'law of averages' prevails over the 'law of aggregation'.*

(iii) *Lack of a nodal Command Authority for Joint Operations. Execution is still through Committees, notwithstanding the Kargil experience.* The debate, as expressed by an interviewee is *'Unity of Effort' v/s 'Unity of Command'.*

(iv) There is little or no synergy between Ministry of Defence and Academic Institutions, Research and Analysis bodies in the evolution of government policy. *Decision making hence not fully informed and backed by rigorous analysis and policy research tools.*

(v) *Certain procurement decisions, particularly 'blacklisting' taken knee jerk on political considerations* without obtaining from Services an estimate of impact on operational capability which jeopardises national security.

NOTES

1. Singh, Jaswant, 'Defending India' Palgrave Macmillan, 1999, p. 41.
2. Gen. Malik, V.P., *India's Military Conflicts and Diplomacy: An Inside view of Decision Making* (Harper Collins Publishers, 2013), p. 256.
3. Ibid.

4. Malik, op. cit., pp. 256-7.
5. Mukherjee, Anit, *Defense Planning in India: Role of Civil–Military Relations*, IDSA.
6. Cowshish, Amit, 'Financial Management in Defence: The Indian Experience', *India Strategic*, July 2011 Edition.
7. 'How Sanjay Gandhi Interviewed an Admiral for a Top Post', *The Times of India*, 28 Nov 2014 (Bangalore Edition).
8. Nanavatty, Rostum K, *Internal Armed Conflict in India: Forging a Joint Civil Military Approach*, by CLAWS & Pentagon Press.

CHAPTER 9

DISCORD AND MISTRUST

LACK OF ADEQUATE INTEREST FROM POLITICAL CLASS

One aspect on which senior present and past functionaries across the 'Civil' and 'Military' divide agreed was that notwithstanding periodic rhetoric and loud averments of praise and support for the Armed Forces, the overall levels of interest in the political class regarding matters concerning national security are abysmally low. A consensus emerged that at any time, not more than a handful of political personages of standing have demonstrated an abiding and continuing quest for an in-depth understanding on matters relating to national security.

As emphasised by Nitin Gokhale, Security and Strategic Affairs Editor, NDTV, '*The political executive, barring a handful few, neither has the knowledge nor any interest in matters military and, therefore, depends completely on inputs from the bureaucrats who continue to mould the political leadership's thought process according to their own perceptions on governance and administration.*'[1] Evolving policy on national security issues calls for an in-depth understanding not just about threat perceptions and military capabilities, it also requires a wide understanding of geo-politics, diplomacy, economics and finance and hence involves effort, perhaps to extents and levels that hectic schedules of members of the political class would not allow them to spare.

Admiral Arun Prakash, has written that '*two major factors have contributed to the systemic dysfunctionality that we see in the management of national security affairs.* ***First is the politician's detachment and indifference towards matters relating to national security, because this is not an issue that can win or lose votes.*** *Since politicians have not considered it worthwhile establishing close and cordial relations with the leadership of the Armed Forces, it is not surprising that when faced with a crisis or a problem, politicians find themselves to be at a complete loss. A related factor is the total reliance the politician places for advice, decision making and problem resolution, on transient, generalist MoD Civil Servants, drawn from diverse backgrounds. This, despite the Chiefs and the highly specialised SHQ Staffs being at his disposal for tendering advice in the management of national security.*'[2]

Admiral Arun Prakash's view is endorsed by another former Service Chief, Gen S Padmanabhan who quotes from his own experiences that '*Even at the level of the Defence Minister and Service Chiefs, exchanges on major matters of defence policy were few and far between, the Defence Minister's Weekly Meetings with the Service Chiefs being used to update the Minister and equip him to negotiate questions in Parliament. Often these meetings were deferred as 'more important' activities claimed the time of the Minister.... The result was...the greater role and authority assumed by the Defence bureaucracy. The Defence Secretary, with his nearness to the Defence Minister, often began to exercise power on the Minister's behalf and was, quite often, regarded as de facto Defence Minister*'. Resultantly, General Padmanabhan adds, '*the supremacy of the civil over the military was thus, effectively changed from supremacy of the political authority to that of the civilian bureaucracy.*'[3]

While accepting there being less than adequate interest in the political class regarding security matters, the Civil side argument is that those in the political class who have shown interests have done so to remarkable extents, asking sharp questions and engaging in threadbare discussions. Decisions of the political authority are eventually well considered ones, taken after careful evaluation of pros and cons. In that, their own (civil servants') role is crucial and they have been playing that role satisfactorily.

Apart from this one aspect, there is little confluence between the perceptions of how past and present senior military men and bureaucrats perceive the present state of matters. Some apprehensions expressed on the two sides of the divide are as discussed below.

THE MILITARY'S CONCERNS

On Implementation of Group of Ministers' Recommendations

Services Officials welcomed and accepted the recommendations made in the Group of Ministers Report. Some felt that had these been accepted and recommended, the grievances and shortcomings that continue to plague the functioning of the Military would have been resolved and the Civil–Military debate in India would perhaps have settled. Those in the know considered the NCTF recommendations to be a substantial dilution though some opined that even accepting those would be forward movement to a half-way house. The delay in accepting even the NCTF recommendations is an indicator to the enormous clout of the bureaucracy to hold their turf and their power to guide the political leadership.

A few, mainly Air Force officers, however, strongly expressed that the present system as stabilised now was 'fine' and that large-scale systemic changes would not by themselves enhance military effectiveness. Naval Officers were ambivalent in their stand, with some accepting that 'Jointness' was an inevitability. In the words of one senior Naval interviewee '*whatever the Services do, it is important they think, plan and press jointly*' mentioning *that 'by itself, the Navy would not be able to do much to dent policy'.*

A view was also expressed that the *bureaucrats have been able to safeguard their turf by sowing doubts into the Navy and Air Force, who being 'smaller' Services* were nudged into the fear of being 'dominated' and 'swamped' by the Army.

On HQ IDS

The creation of HQ IDS and its functioning, has been a very positive futuristic reform and functional integration of the Services being inevitable in the time to come. There was also a contrary view of *the three Armed Forces and their various components being specific cadres with their own respective specialisations. If an Institutional structure brings about an end state in which the edge of specialisation comes to be blunted instead of sharpened, it is not serving its purpose. HQ IDS, though manned by officers from all the three Forces has come to be an additional layer of a 'generalist' form of a 'uniformed' bureaucratic layer between Services HQs and the Ministry of Defence with a working principle better expressed in the words of a former Air Force Officer is of 'applying the law of averages'.*

A senior Armed Forces officer conceded that the three Services had each conducted reviews of how HQ IDS was serving its purpose but each eventually felt that in balance it did so within its limitations. In any case, as one retired Officer mentioned 'it is a clock that cannot now be put back'. Another apprehension on a practical plane is that *serving Service Chief would be extremely unwilling to accept being divested of his own authority and reduce his role to a status of a planner, recruiter and supporter of theatre commanders.* They would prefer to remain smug in their respective roles and continue the 'pretence of maintaining a *plastic sham jointness*'.

An irksome administrative issue was also raised. *As career prospects in the three services being different, promotions to equivalent ranks is not in tandem.* This has led to anomalous situations where a 'senior' from one Service finds himself as a functional or positional subordinate to a 'junior' from another Service. (This issue should correctly have been foreseen and resolved at the time HQ IDS was raised).

ON COUNTERING SERVICE-SPECIFIC THREATS

Some Army Officers strongly felt that on matters relating to **LIC and IS** there is really little on which a 'non-Army' Commander-in-Chief could effectively contribute at the highest decision making levels and that *operational aspects on such 'only Army' issues should be left entirely to the Army.*

At junior levels, some apprehensions were expressed that the entire 'scheme' of creating new structures and proliferation of appointments was intended to enhance promotion prospects in senior ranks, that too only in certain cadres (The Infantry and Artillery in the Army, The Executive Cadre of the Navy and Fighter Pilots).

THE BUREAUCRATS' VIEWPOINTS

On Inclusion of Military in Decision Making

The bureaucracy overwhelmingly did not share the Military's perceptions on its claim to be given a formal role in policy formulation and decision making. They instead considered that security decisions are, in essence and nature, 'political' and/or 'diplomatic'. Military inputs to arrive at these decisions, though important are but one in a range of factors upon which decisions are based. The Military they stressed, is already providing requisite inputs and the mechanisms for obtaining its inputs and recommendations are robust and time tested. No added advantage would obtain by formally including the Military into the decision making structures. As one retired bureaucrat candidly opined, 'policy formulation is akin to gourmet cooking – each ingredient towards its formulation is required to be carefully selected, analysed, its veracity doubly ensured, its relevance evaluated in the matrix of other inputs. The provider of any one ingredient does not elevate to being the Chef. That is another profession'.

The Bureaucrat's Role

Shri NS Sisodia, erstwhile Director IDSA and a former Additional Secretary in the Ministry of Defence puts the same argument somewhat differently, distinguishing the roles of the bureaucrat and the political decision maker. In his words, 'nowhere in the world, even on the military side...are directives given by the political executive. What the political executives do is to consider options which are placed before them. If they have a political preference of any kind from their own perspective, they will express it in their decision. But they cannot be expected to write down even an operational directive or any kind of national security strategy. This is a job for officials to do'.[4]

Limitations of Military's Administrative Abilities

The Military, though an efficient organisation with clockwork executive skills, does not inherently possess superior administrative skills on matters outside of concern to their own Services. It is neither trained nor experienced to manage financial matters particularly at the macro level. Mention was made of a tendency to overspend and profligate on the part of CFAs from the Services that have been curtailed by determined and watchful IFAs which institution the Defence Services views to be an impediment.

Prior consultation with military before issuance of an executive direction has always been a norm. If studied closely, the failure of the military to execute directions are attributable not so much to infirmities in directions given to the Military but rather to the Military's own failure either to assess the magnitude of the operational task or to overestimate their own capabilities which as one bureaucrat puts it are 'two sides of the same coin'.

The Civil side argues that the military is a body of professionals, 'more like medical and computer specialists'. The segregation of policy formulation from execution of military actions is, according to some bureaucrats, the very essence of civilian control of the military which, in the words of one senior bureaucrat 'should not, wholly or partly, play a role in determining its own actions'.

A view was expressed on the side of the Bureaucracy that 'policy formulation (and decision making) at Government level cannot and should not be viewed as akin to or an extension of military decision making'. It is a deliberate process that includes factors beyond the scope of the military including alternate costs for the fiscal resources expended in military actions as also the political intent and inclinations of the leadership. These are aspects best left out of the realm of the Military to evaluate and recommend choices.

If given a place on the decision making high table, the Military would require expending much time and energy into understanding a wide range of issues and subjects not directly related to their prime professional field which may, however, be 'bread and butter' issues for a bureaucrat. The existing system in any case provides for both the Military and the civil side to place their respective considered advice, inputs and opinion, as based upon their professional experience and expertise, before the Political Authority. That, in the perception of the bureaucracy, is suffice.

Issues of Style and Attitude

A senior bureaucrat stressed upon a tendency in the Military top echelons to be 'obsessed with "self-opinion' on strategic issues and dismissive of everyone else's viewpoints' as being an impediment to a balanced Civil–Military relationship. On the practical side, bureaucrats argue that if the Military were to be given a formal place on the decision making 'high table', the 'purposeful' role it would facilitate shall still restrict to providing its inputs and assessments, which are in any case being obtained from them under the existing system. **What may result is that the Military gets drawn into discussions and debates on issues which are in the realm of 'political' matters and thereby impinge on the strictly 'apolitical' character of the Armed Forces which is not desirable.** The existing 'silent practice' of 'prior consultation' before issuance of formal Government executive Orders provides an added 'safety fuse' to the Military leadership to once again express itself on the 'executability' of important decisions before they are formally issued.

Another aspect stressed by Bureaucrats is the vast differential in the 'administrative culture' between the civil and military sides. **Military decisions are invariably 'top-down' the role of a 'sub-leadership' functionary is to treat a superior's viewpoint or opinion as 'bounden' and a 'given'.** The civil side works on a more consultative style with all levels of the processing hierarchy having full unencumbered freedom and opportunity to express views/opinions on a proposal. The endorsements of each of these functionaries stays on file and is available for reference and/or scrutiny at a later stage. **An exposure of Services personnel to**

such a decision-making mechanism would be against the grain of the 'superior' – 'subordinate' functional ethos of the Defence Forces.

NOTES

1. Gokhale, Nitin, 'Defence Management in India: Need for Urgent Reappraisal', CLAWS Journal, Summer 2013.
2. Gokhale, op. cit., p. 14.
3. Padmanabhan, S., *A General Speaks* (New Delhi: Manas Publications, 2005), p. 109.
4. Proceedings of USI Seminar on Higher Defence Management held at USI on 24-25 August 2006.

CHAPTER 10

REDEFINING THE CIVIL–MILITARY BALANCE

THE WAY FORWARD

The cardinal finding of this book is that there is no dispute whatsoever on the aspect of civilian control over the military being a cornerstone of the edifice of democracy. The Military, however, emphasises that Civilian here is the political authority and not the bureaucrat. Issues the Military raises to question the efficacy of the existing system are:

(a) Does the regimen of a 'generalist' control meet the requirements of national security in present-day context?
(b) Is the 'expertise' of the military, its experience, and knowledge and career-long association with matters of security being effectively utilised in decision making and policy formulation?
(c) Would a participative inclusion of the military in the decision-making process that will enrich the quality of decision making agitate against 'democratic principles'?

Today's obtaining security situation requires quick, effective decisions to counter emergent situations. A clear visualisation and assessment of issues is an imperative. The critical need is to draw up the alternatives or options for implementation. These decisions involve deployment and utilisation of scarce national human resource and assets, besides having a bearing on national security. Directions emanating from such decisions must therefore necessarily be achievable with the best amongst available options being directed for implementation.

A number of proposals and/or suggestions have been put forward from time to time by various Committees as correctives to the system and in procedures. *What is required is that the respective roles of both, the Civil and importantly, the military, be made clear and transparent so as to define clearly the contours within which each, particularly the latter, functions.* There is no gainsaying that issues involved concern the entire national military-security apparatus and are far too complex to be seen through a simplistic 'us vs them' prism.

Bereft of rhetoric, some of the suggestions made on the side of the Military are:

(a) **Need for a clear, holistic visualisation of 'Comprehensive National Power' (CNP) and the role of Military therein.** The objectives to be achieved by the military should be clearly and unambiguously expostulated and disseminated to the general public. Military service as generally regarded, is a sacred national service which the youth of our country are encouraged to join. ***It is a profession that calls for a lifetime commitment. In today's day and age, it is not right to spin a dream to attract our youth to make a commitment without informing them upfront of what the nature of the service is and importantly, what the call of their profession is, the skills it imparts, how these skills are to utilised to meet national objectives. Today's youth are a pragmatic entity with sharp ability to conceptualise realities and they need to be appropriately informed.***

(b) **Cogent 'doctrinal' articulation on the use of Military as 'an instrument of power to meet national objectives.** The example of Russia's Military Doctrine (available in the public domain) is often mentioned as the appropriate form of public statement that expounds in clear lucid terms the role of the military, its professional objectives and its command and control structure. A similar document would define the contours of respective areas of professional functioning for all stakeholders be it the political authority, bureaucrat, diplomat or the soldier.

(c) **A comprehensive national security architecture that harnesses professional capabilities, domain knowledge and experience of all**

professions including the military. In the existing system, the military feels substantively excluded from the decision-making process. It sees its contributions to be at best, indirect and feels perturbed that bureaucrats who are neither formally or extensively trained or informed on matters of strategy 'call the shots' without adequate grasp of complexities and operational constraints. This, it is feared, can lead to a disastrous mismatch between identifying a problem and issuing directions, the most quoted example being the disjointed and ill-informed one in 1962 when the then Prime Minister directed the Army to 'evict the Chinese from Indian territory' in abject disregard to and obvious ignorance of the state of the Army's preparedness for the enormity of the operation. ***What the Military dreads most is a political decision made in haste – particularly one which could catch national imagination and in today's media driven public opinion, raise national emotion and expectations from the Armed Forces pushing them into 'playing a match' against the grain of their own capacity to achieve success.***

A MILITARY COMMAND STRUCTURE THAT IS EMPOWERED IN BUILDING ITS OWN CAPACITIES WITH A VOICE TO RENDER ITS FRANK PROFESSIONAL ADVICE

Notwithstanding who makes the eventual decisions and gives directions, military knows it carries the onus of accountability and responsibility for operational failures. Here again, the need for fair opportunity being given to the Military to express its professional assessments and cautions is underscored.

EMPOWERING MILITARY COMMANDERS

Once the civil authority has given its decision /directions to the military, the 'follow up' to execute must thereafter rest solely with the military. For this, the roles of the Service Chiefs and Chairman COSC both as advisors, planners and executors of military operations require to be clearly defined. ***This empowerment should be by way of granting them requisite administrative authority and their respective roles sanctified with the inclusion of their roles in the AoB and ToB Rules.***

INTEGRATION WITH MoD

The Military sees some hope in the various proposals made by the Group of Ministers and by the Naresh Chandra Task Force. Though the recommendations of the latter are widely perceived by the military to be merely cosmetic, yet achieving even the half-way house, in present circumstances, is a move forward. What the Services seek is in essence, their inclusion as an integral part of the national government superstructure. They see themselves playing arduous and difficult roles to overcome situations that the civil administration had been unable to handle at times of national crisis, yet being told off by a mid-runged Ministry of Defence bureaucrat that they are "gazetted only by the Ministry of Defence and not by the DOPT". Hardly pleasant to the ears of one posted to the Services HQ after a difficult field posting. As expressed by one serving officer, *'the Army marches on its "izzat" for a longer distance than it marches on its stomach'.* Systemic fault lines that dissipate this *'izzat'* need urgent rectification.

Posting of Service Officers to the Ministry of Defence. The paucity of domain knowledge in the Ministry of Defence, especially in operations related Divisions is obvious. While 'inputs' are no doubt obtained from the concerned Branches of the Services HQs, a stage of analysis follows where raw untrained non-military minds 'process' the information to formulate options for action or policies. In either case, having Services personnel on their Staff as 'captive' advisors would firstly facilitate better functional liaison, facilitate a knowledgeable mind to apply itself to the information and satisfy to its completeness and relevance and above all, assist in the formulation of options. The threat of the Services 'creeping' in to the Ministry of Defence is misplaced as decision making would always remain squarely with the Civilian Authority.

Single File System: One not-so-radical change that reckons immediate implementation is the introduction of a 'Single File System' as in fact had existed in the past. This would in itself enable Services HQ to better integrate into the decision-making loop through understanding the rationale underlying decisions without compromising the authority of the designated 'Competent Authority'.

Need for a Specialist Cadre of Defence Administrators: The harshest opinions on the side of the Services were, however, reserved for the attitude, behaviour and conduct of the junior bureaucracy of the Ministry of Defence. Most senior Services Officer interacted with bore no grudge against the senior bureaucracy, their commitment and hard work. One former Service Chief even mentioned his observing that senior bureaucrats perhaps worked for longer hours than their Military counterparts and were at their desks even on holidays. Though there may be differences and the bureaucracy had its limitations, interaction with them was invariably pleasant. The 'bane', in the perception of the Military is at the mid and junior executive levels where 'Precedence is King and Conservatism the Rule'.

The knowledge base, rules, regulations, procedures, systems, traditions of service, etc., that lie at the core of decision making on defence and security matters is a specialised field, substantially different from that in vogue in other Government Departments. A strong case exists for an informed, specially trained and committed bureaucracy across the Defence Ministry and the Services Headquarters manned by a set of dedicated professional executive staff. Their understanding and inputs would vastly enhance the quality of analysis over that of the present-day generalists allocated to the Defence Ministry under Central Staffing.

The Arun Singh Task Force has recommended a dedicated Civilian Specialist cadre to cater to Security and Strategic issues. **A Defence Administrative Service panning appointments across the Ministry of Defence, Service HQs and even Command Headquarters as also emerging establishments such as the INDU is an imperative. The role of the AFHQ Civil Service can be redefined and its cadres managed, trained and redeployed to this end.**

Standardising Working Procedures. If the eventual aim to achieve is for the Services Headquarters being designated Departments of the Government, then administrative and decision making procedures followed in these Headquarters must conform, as far as possible, to Government Rules, Regulations and Procedures as followed across various Civil Ministries and Departments. The Whitehall Filing System in vogue in the Services HQ would need a review.

Substantive Jointness within the Services. While on the one side Services have been urging appropriate institutional and procedural changes to enable their being included in the decision making structures and processes, certain constraining factors lie within their own domain. Here the Services have to accept some part of the blame as some or other of them as at various times, one or other of them have resisted significant reforms to infuse substantial Jointness such as instituting a common 'Armed Forces Act', common and procedures, joint administrative structures and command and control systems. *Even on issues of common tri-service concern, such as the Pay Commission issues, in the words of a senior officer, 'they choose to work together, but not as one'.*

DEFENCE PROCUREMENT POLICY

This discussion would be incomplete without due reference to the positives of reforms in Defence Procurement. The Procedures for Defence procurement had been laid down in 1992, but post-recommendations of the Group of Ministers' Report in 2000, a comprehensively reviewed and revised Defence Procurement Procedure had been introduced in December 2002. Thereafter, the scope of these procedures has been revised and enlarged through periodical reviews resulting in the promulgation of the DPP 2003, 2005, 2006, 2008, 2011, 2013 and most recently, in April 2016. The extant policy is inclusive and transparent harnessing the domain expertise of the Services, the Scientist, the Finance Experts with coordination and oversight provided by the bureaucrats. The procedure details the various steps to be followed at each stage of the procurement process and adopts a 'Committee' approach especially at crucial stages like categorisation to the final approval for procurement. Voices are no doubt heard of the procedures being long-winding, but few fault its fairness and transparency.

A notable feature that spins out of this Policy is appointing Technical Managers from the Defence Services in the Acquisition Wing of the Ministry of Defence. ***This arrangement, which has been in place for over a decade and finds acceptance on both the Civil and Military sides, is an effective demonstrator of why similar arrangements to harness the experience of Services Officers into other Ministry of Defence Departments could serve an equally effective and purposeful role.***

Conclusion

Civilian Control of the Military and the nature of CMR lie at the core of a democracy system of Government. There is no debate that in a democracy, the Military should be controlled by the duly elected Civilian Authority, and effectively so. The Military serves a unique and cardinal purpose. There is no substitute to it for the role it executes. *Democracy, unguarded by an effective military, is hollow.*

Control mechanisms over the military must therefore promote and support the development and sustenance of an effective military force that enables and ensures, at all times, the most robust credible defence to its people. Existing control mechanisms are bureaucrat controlled and managed. While from the 'Civilian' Controller's perspective the extent of control is effective and required, it is stifling and counter-productive from that of the controlled 'Military'.

These are times when the nature of threats is changing. The emergence of non-state actors, the nature of asymmetrical warfare they resort to call for rapid responses required to be taken on a near real-time basis. The immediate professional assessment of the Military becomes the core determinant upon which such decisions would be based. *The old Da-Vinci model of 'natural' (civil) administrators who can 'grasp all the essentials of every complex military situation and suggest quick fix solutions' and possess a breadth of vision and a penchant 'to see the larger picture' of each emerging situation in the context of its overarching matrix, simply does not exist anymore.*

To enable they do so, it is essential to base the decision making structure on a platform which is supported by both, the 'genius of the administrator' as also the 'technical expertise of the military'. For the civil administrator to show his genius there is a requirement that he be in direct functional contact with the military specialist at every stage of decision making and include the participation of the latter in policy formulation. The onus of attaining the most robust balance of expertise between them and the Military lies squarely on the Civilian Authority.

Direct participation of the Military in apex level decision making or even it being given an advocacy role in the higher decision making would, as a norm, agitate against the essence of the democratic traditions. The Military's role in the apex decision making process, at all stages, should restrict to being advisory. Having stipulated that, it is in the national interest that the Civilian Authority provide the Military with the fullest possible opportunity to provide required facts and put forth its assessments.

While disagreement on the part of the Military is not necessarily dissent, it needs to be duly understood on its part of there being limits to pressing forth a contrary viewpoint. Its pleadings, as mentioned before, must be based on facts and professional assessments and expressed without animosity, rancour or casting doubts on the competence and ability of the decision makers. The red line for the Military expressing itself is that once decisions are taken and directions issued, its role is to execute the directions given to it to the best of its professional capability. In present day context, this red line must extend to subterfuge through selective media leaks or leveraging media in any way whatsoever to build public information or disinformation against directions given to it.

This perceived 'bane' of the Civilian Controllers having less than adequate knowledge and understanding of Military matters and capabilities must be frontally addressed by providing them requisite exposure through training programmes and specialist training capsules on the one hand and to include Military experts into their hierarchies who can provide 'hands on' expert assistance and guidance that would contribute to informed decision making.

In his article "Improving Civil Military Relations", Ganapathy Vanchinathan, Senior Fellow at the Centre for Land Warfare Studies brings out that over the decades, several *committees have been constituted and reports prepared for the cause of defence reforms, right from the time of independence when Prime Minister Jawaharlal Nehru commissioned Patrick Blacket, British Military Consultant and Scientist to help 'Indianise the Military'.* Vanchinathan goes on the emphasise that *"significantly, all these (Committees) have underscored the need for integration of the civilian and military functionaries, with the obvious underlying intent of developing trust amongst each other. Without moving forward on this front, enacting or implementing other reforms would be like giving shape to a body, but without a soul. There is thus a need to identify institutional ways to create, build, foster and maintain trust between the civilian and military functionaries."*[1]

The surmise of this effort is an emphasis on the need for an early rebalance of the Civil–Military functional relationship to place it on an even keel to enable a smooth glide into a possible tumultuous future that would require all agencies of Government to work in harmony and tandem.

NOTE

1. 'Improving Civil Military Relations' by Ganapathy Vanchinathan CLAWS 18 February 2014 @http://www.claws.in/1153/improving-civil-military-relations-ganapathy-vanchinathan.html

SELECT BIBLIOGRAPHY

'A General Speaks' by General S Padmanabhan (Manas Publications).

'A Tale of Two Aruns' by Inder Malhotra (*The Hindu*, 17 May 2000).

'Armed Forces in British India' by Rajkumar Pruthi & Rameshwari Devi (Pointer Publishers) 1998.

Beaumont, Roger, *Sword of the Raj*, New York: The Bob Merill Company Ltd, 1977.

'British Policy in India 1858–1905' by S Gopal (Cambridge University Press) 1965.

Central Secretariat Manual of Office Procedure (issued by Department of Personnel & Administrative Reforms, Government of India).

Chiding the Chiefs – Political Leaders have undermined Military Morale by Lt Gen (Retd) Harwant Singh (http://generalharwants.blogspot.in/2011/01/chiding-chiefs.html).

Civil–Military Relations: A Comparative Study of India and Pakistan by Kotera M. Bhimaya (RAND Graduate School Publication).

Civilian Control' by Richard Kohn (*American Diplomacy* magazine, 2012 Issue)

'Defending India' by Jaswant Singh (Macmillan).

'Internal Armed Conflict in India: Forging a Joint Civil-Military Approach' by Rostum K Nanavatty (CLAWS & Pentagon Press).

'India's Military Conflicts and Diplomacy: An Inside view of Decision Making' by Gen VP Malik (Harper Collins).

'Is Izzat-o-Iqbal?' by Admiral Arun Prakash. (http://www.livefistdefence.com/2008/06/exclusive-concluding-thoughts-by.html).

'Issues of Democracy: Civil Military Relations in a Democracy'. (*Electronic Journals of the US Information Agency*, July 1997, Vol. 2, No. 3).

'Indian Army through the Ages' by Major Gautam Sharma (Allied Publishers Pvt Ltd), 1966.

'Inside the Indian Army' by Brig Trigunesh Mukherjee (Manas Publications), 2000.

'India and its Armies' by Stephen Peter Rosen (Oxford University Press), 1996.

'Indian Defence Forces: The Turning Points' by Ranbir Singh & Ranjit Kumar Mandal (Krutika Books, New Delhi), 2002.

'India's Defence Problem' by SS Khera (Orient Longman)

'John Company: Indian and Pakistan Armies 1903-1991' by John Gaylor (Lancer Publishers), 1993.

'KM Cariappa : His Life and Times' by Brig CB Khanduri (Atlas Books) 1995.

'Military System of Independent India' by Raj Kumar (Commonwealth Publishers).

Restructuring and Integration of the Ministry of Defence with the Three Service Headquarters by Lt Gen Satish Nambiar (USI National Security Paper 2012).

'The Military System in India 1900-1939' by Dr KML Saxena (Reliance Publishing House, New Delhi) 1999.

'The Indian Army' by Stephen Cohen (Oxford University Press) 1990.

Transformation of the Armed Forces: 2025 Enhancing India's Defence by Dr AK Lal.

Thirty Second Report of the Standing Committee on Defence (2008-09) Lok Sabha Secretariat.

The Government of India Allocation of Business Rules (issued January 14, 1961 by the President's Secretariat).

INDEX